PARENTS
FOREVER

PARENTS
FOREVER

You and Your Adult Children

Sidney Callahan

CROSSROAD • NEW YORK

1992

The Crossroad Publishing Company
370 Lexington Avenue, New York, NY 10017

Copyright © 1992 by Sidney Callahan

Printed in the United States of America

Library of Congress Cataloging-in-Publication Data

Callahan, Sidney Cornelia.
    Parents forever : you and your adult children / Sidney Callahan.
      p.   cm.
    ISBN 0-8245-1195-6
    1. Parent and adult child—United States.   2. Intergenerational
relations—United States.   I. Title.
HQ755.86.C35   1992
306.874—dc20   92-9762
                                                    CIP

I dedicate this book to
Virginia W. Eldridge,
with love, admiration, and gratitude
for the half-century and more
that she has been a good mother to me.

And to my husband, Dan, and our children,
Mark, Stephen, John, Peter, Sarah, and David,
who made this book possible.

Contents

CHAPTER ONE

When Does It Ever End?

"They never told us it would go on so long!" Middle-aged parents, with offspring in their twenties and thirties, can be by turns surprised, challenged, befuddled, exasperated, and bewildered by their adult children. "Is there ever an end to our responsibility?" they ask. Or to put it more crassly, "When can we stop sending money?"

Financial support, however, is only one of the puzzles parents of adults face. Questions about work, sex, values, and how to handle conflict come up as well. Not all parents meet the same situations or have the same kind of concerns, but there is a lot of parental worrying going on in our society.

I write this book to assure parents of adults that they are not alone in their uncertainties. Something new seems to be happening: Launching children into adulthood and living with them ever after is not what it used to be. While Erma Bombeck's columns let us chuckle over the new conditions parents face, there have been few focused discussions on this newest example of a "problem without a name."

Can we name this problem? Yes, I think so. Many parents of adults are confronting turbulent new cultural currents and social conditions without any tried-and-true guidelines for their actions. There is little consensus about what the parental role should be once children are young adults. What is a parent's moral obligation to adult children and what can parents expect from them in turn?

It doesn't help much to look for guidance from social science research because research always lags behind social change and never addresses questions of moral responsibility. I know, because I am a social psychologist who has been reading and writing about the family for decades, but I have found little in the professional literature that could help me sort out dilemmas with my own children. My children(?!) — however inappropriate the word we seem stuck with it — range from their midtwenties to their midthirties. Like so many other middle-aged parents of our generation my husband and I are surprised to find how involved we still are with their lives and how many puzzles they present.

I am addressing my own uncertainties in this book, but I have also drawn upon the experiences of many others. Every story and quote from a parent or adult child in this book is real, although I have disguised the names of the speakers. I have also found novels and stories to be a fruitful source of apt material. Literature and art, along with religious writing, can illuminate subtle and morally nuanced concerns and emotions that parents experience. By mid-life men and women are not so bound by the rigid sex role pressures of early child rearing, so I include comments and concerns of both mothers and fathers.

In this attempt to reflect on present-day parents and their adult children I am using everything I can to help make sense of a confusing scene — distilling professional resources that have been both expanded and honed by personal interest. After all I'm a player in the game as well as a critical observer.

As a parent I write from the parent's point of view, taking the parent's perspective. Other books address adult children who want to deal with past family experiences that are still affecting their adult lives. Many groups exist for adult children of alcoholics or other family survivors who must come to terms with their parents. There are fewer books or groups for parents in the middle passage who feel beleaguered trying to come to terms with their adult children.

But why are parents finding themselves in troubled waters? In my own case part of the difficulty comes from a past that did not adequately prepare me for parenthood. When I started out thirtysome years ago I was an optimistic American innocent (educated female division), setting out with quite unrealistic ideas about family living.

I had only the most sketchy picture of baby care, courtesy of Dr. Spock's early editions. From my own middle-class childhood as the eldest of two sisters, I had garnered a few other vague ideas about providing after-school cookies and milk, sewing Halloween costumes and the need for a nutritious diet. But because I had been a good girl, bent on making my parents proud of me by my precocious adult behavior, I had no premonitions of any troubles that might occur during childhood or the adolescent period!

Looking back on my early view of parenthood, I also see that I assumed my children would go to college, with our financial help. But the pictures in my head of college graduation were clearly marked, THE END, FINIS, no more parenting required. The next family scenarios flitting through my youthful head were flashforwards to a deathbed scene, in which I dispensed jewels and pearls of wisdom to my assembled children and grandchildren. (I had been reading the copious Renaissance literature on death and dying in the Shakespeare library where I worked.)

What was missing? There were no expectations of a period when I would be a middle-aged adult and my children also would be adults. Perhaps this blank existed because in your twenties it is almost impossible to imagine yourself as middle aged. In his golden youth F. Scott Fitzgerald once wrote of a "faded but still lovely woman of twenty-eight;" at twenty-two the idea of being fifty something is more or less unimaginable. At any rate everyone else in my generation also believed that parenthood would be over and done with when one's children graduated from college.

Like many women I knew I left home at eighteen, married in college, and had a large brood of children by thirty-two. We rushed enthusiastically into adult commitments and heavy family responsibilities. My husband and I moved far away from our families and never came home again, except for brief visits. (Who wants to see you coming with three babies in diapers or with six children under ten?) As an independent young wife and mother far from home and on my own, I was busy being the center of my own world. I never asked my parents for help and would never think of sharing my problems with them. I had no clue that parents either could or would continue to function as parents beyond anyone's twenty-first birthday.

But no matter how knowledgeable I might have been in the 1950s, could I or anyone else in that era ever have predicted the events coming in future decades? Society has undergone seismic shifts in cultural and economic conditions in the last thirty years. Who could have foreseen Vietnam, urban riots, hippies, the sexual revolution, new medical technologies, Watergate and runaway epidemics of drugs, divorce, and AIDS? Social, religious and political upheavals have been followed by economic recessions. Not a likely scenario during the Eisenhower years.

Another crucial development is our new realization of what increasing life expectancies will bring in an aging population. With extended longevity parents and their children may share fifty to sixty years of life together. Never has a period of parenthood between the birth of one's children and one's own death extended for so long. More to the point — thanks to modern health care and affluence — never have so many parents lived so many decades as healthy vigorous middle-aged adults alongside their offspring who are also healthy vigorous young adults. Middle-aged people don't act old anymore; they engage in youthful activities much like their adult children, including sex. Have parents and children ever jogged together before, or belonged to the same health clubs? Or dressed the same, and talked about the same movies or TV shows?

Two generations now can exist together in the prime of adult life for three decades; this extended time produces many new potential twists and turns in the parent-child relationship. Yet most of the books on parents and family life are devoted to the beginning and the end, the alpha and omega, of the life cycle. When you go to your neighborhood bookstore you find a long shelf of baby-care and child-care books, followed by a few books devoted to helping parents survive their children's adolescence.

The next cluster of family books changes perspective and focus; these omega books are devoted to the end of life and aimed at helping middle-aged individuals cope with the needs of their old parents. There are never any books about how parents should deal with their adult children *before* that last stage of life — so I have included a chapter on mid-life parental preparations for old age, illness, and death, or how to cope with your old age better than King Lear.

But a lot of issues come up in the decades when parents and their adult children are both living as vigorous adults. Here there is almost nothing written except for a few problem centered books — your adult child as an alcoholic, or as a schizophrenic — or coming to terms with your son's homosexuality and the scourge of AIDS. Dramatic problems do abound but there is little discussion of the general character of the parent-adult child relationship and more ordinary interactions. And there is almost nothing about the positive new possibilities for friendship and cooperation that an extended life together in good health can bring to a family.

If ripeness is all, American parents and their adult children now share a goodly amount of prime time. In fact, one of the things many parents of adult children are unprepared for is the fun, friendship, and companionship they experience with their adult children. This is the nice part of the surprise package delivered to our generation.

Many other surprises emerge, I am sure, because rapid social changes have left our cultural images of family life out of phase with social reality. Dick, Jane, and Spot don't depict modern childhood and Norman Rockwell's depictions of family gatherings no longer apply. Moreover, structural factors built into extended middle stages of parenthood may make it harder to construct general norms for either mothers or fathers. Variety, individuality, and specificity can characterize a parent-adult child relationship. When two persons are each independently functioning adults, they can voluntarily negotiate or renegotiate the relationship that is going to exist between them. (Many parents and adult children may be caught in left-over patterns and compulsions from childhood, but it doesn't have to be that way if one party won't play his or her role in the game.)

When neither parent nor child is dependent upon the other for sustenance or care, then their mutual independence can result in a diversity of relationships. Parents and their adult children can relate in numerous different patterns — all the way from daily intimacy in a common household to distant residences on different continents.

By contrast we know what dependency at the beginning and at the end of family life requires. Infants and children have similar needs always and everywhere — protection, care, education. For their part, fragile, ill, and aged parents also have needs for care and support. Our culture has always maintained that responsible, morally mature adults in their prime should nurture their dependent children and care for their old parents.

These social norms for the beginning and end of family life may not always be lived up to, but the norms are clear. We believe in responsible parenthood and filial piety. But what is supposed to happen in the newly extended middle stage of family living? If each member of the parent-child dyad is independent, what kind of interdependence or family relations ought to be worked out? And on what grounds? Many do not know what parents and their adult children owe each other, if anything. Many of us who have moved away from our cultural and ethnic roots are not sure. We are making it up as we go along, from day to day, from situation to situation.

It has to be recognized however, that I speak for only one segment of today's middle-aged parents. America is composed of many different folks living in different parts of the country with diverse traditions. In many communities families are still quite sure of how things are "supposed to be" between parents and their adult children. Some family traditions have not been disrupted by uprooting, family breakdown, or mobility — I think here of certain settled communities in the Midwest. In many places, like Grand Rapids for instance, the traditional customs and rules of parent-child behavior over the life cycle have not been disturbed. You may work with your parents on the farm or in the shop, or work near your parents; you may live downstairs or across town,

and everyone shows up for Sunday dinner and holidays. Most social life in the United States takes place in family celebrations and
gatherings.

Asian and Hispanic immigrant groups also bring with them established family customs of common work and residence that resist disruption. All the assured and unruffled parents in smoothly
operating family systems are not going to be impelled to read
this book. Only parents who face unexpected new conditions,
uncertainties, crises, and downturns in family life will feel that
for them the solid foundations and traditions of the middle-class
family have been shaken.

But before taking on new puzzles that many of today's parents
face, it is worth taking a moment to map those features in the
parent-adult child landscape that have not changed and cannot
change. These inescapable and necessary challenges exist for all
parents of all adult children always and everywhere; they may be
obvious, but they do provide a background for understanding
what is new and different. So what are necessary challenges for
all parents of adult children?

Parents Need to Accept
That a New Generation Will Take Over

If healthy adult parents coexist with healthy adult children, they
may both be in middle adulthood but there is one difference between them. In the normal course of events, adult children are
on their way up and their parents are on their way down. In the
time left for living, parents are a generation closer to old age,
death, and the finish of the race, while their adult children are
just beginning to run the course.

While parents and children can share a period of equality in
adulthood, the equilibrium and balance of power will not remain
the same indefinitely. The most powerful, vigorous, or successful
parent cannot avoid aging and death. Some overwhelmingly potent characters may not only outperform, but also outlive their
adult progeny, but even a Picasso or a Winston Churchill must

die. Replacement of one generation by the next is the iron law of social and family life.

Fathers and mothers know that they will be superseded in strength, power, health, and beauty. Like the friend of the bridegroom, the parent will decrease as the adult child increases. The next generation will eventually move to center stage. This discrepancy in future prospects between the generations has always been taken into account in human cultures.

The Biblical prescription to "honor your father and mother," and "be patient with your father though his mind fail," recognizes the fact that parents inevitably grow weak and their adult children may be tempted to take advantage of them or shoulder them aside ruthlessly. King David in the Old Testament faced the armed rebellion of his favorite son Absalom who rose up with his followers to overthrow his father — and this was not the first or the last case of tension and conflict over the succession of the next in line.

In a benign system the process of parental displacement by the new generation is not violent but slow and gradual. Today, to use a modern example, it is as though parents see themselves gradually written out of the lead roles in a situation comedy or soap opera. Your diminishing role in the drama shrinks to a minor part in the subsidiary plot line. The younger characters are promoted to the leads and become the new stars of the show.

There is an inevitable shift of power and focus in a family, and this changing of the guard can be a source of happiness for parents or the cause of resentment. Parents can feel competitive, envious, and angry over their adult children's growing influence and prowess, or they can take joy in seeing their adult children flourish and grow strong.

The cultural ideal for parents has always been as clear as the admonition to children to honor their parents. While less explicitly voiced, it has been agreed that parents do well to give way graciously and gladly welcome their adult children's ascent to power. An adult child's success should be identified with as a vicarious triumph. Their victory and ascension feeds my happiness. Parents can take comfort and joy that their adult children will live on after them. Their adult children and grandchildren's survival is a touch of immortality to soften the blow of decline and death.

Parents in every flourishing culture have striven to guarantee the social well-being of their adult children; the goal is to have children who will be self-sufficient and able to function successfully as adults. In human societies biological reproduction of offspring is accompanied by parental efforts to position their progeny socially so that they can be empowered to have children of their own. Parental altruism for the second generation is partly aimed at benefiting a third generation of grandchildren.

Selfish interests may also come into play, of course. The more socially powerful one's adult children are, the more assurance a parent may have for good treatment and protection in old age. "My son the doctor," and "my daughter the lawyer," can intimidate the hell out of a hospital and keep health-care workers from getting careless with a vulnerable old body. Highly competent adult children can provide advocacy and protection for an aging parent. Recently the newspapers reported that the attorney son of a sixty-one-year-old mother dismissed from her city job, filed an age discrimination suit on her behalf.

Parents, for all sorts of reasons, keep attempting to provide their children with whatever a society requires for adult competency. Part of the stress for today's parents comes from the confusion over what it may take to make it in our changing society. It was a lot easier when one's duty to the next generation was a matter of passing on basic farming and hunting skills that had always worked well enough for one's ancestors. Yet their own future interests and parental altruism keep parents working for their adult children's ascendancy and well-being. Love, in particular, can overcome competitiveness or envy of the young adult's developing powers — but not always.

One trivial example of the difference between a positive and negative approach to adult children's growing prowess can be seen when parents play tennis with their adult children. (Those readers not convinced of tennis as an analogue of life can substitute another game or activity of their choice.) Anyone who know dedicated competitive tennis players can assure you that th hate to lose. Tennis, like many another game, reveals character and a person's reaction to stress. How do they react to victory, to defeat? Do they cheat?

A parent playing tennis against an adult child may be able to win for many years by relying on greater cunning, self-control, and the concentration given by greater experience. But there will come a day when most adult children will be able to wipe their esteemed parents off the court, filial piety or no. At that point parents can either be proud and happy, identifying with their child's youthful strength and developed skill, or they can give way to resentment. I recall a middle-aged father playing a match against his adult son in a club tennis tournament. The father, who had always been the dominant player, now began to lose. Chagrined, he could not face the prospect of defeat. He began to cheat on his calls and to harass his son verbally — a sad display of excessive personal competitiveness instead of vicarious parental pride.

Envious mothers have also been known to be competitive and express excessive criticisms of their blooming adult daughters. "Mirror, mirror on the wall, who's the fairest of them all," asked Snow White's stepmother. Other ambivalent mothers turn up in novels and in Shirley MacLaine movies. Many women who lived in an era when they were denied educational opportunities or access to satisfying careers may be tempted to resent their daughter's greater good fortune.

A daughter who has social, sexual, and familial success, along with career satisfactions can provoke maternal envy. But a mother who vicariously identifies with her adult daughter can take satisfaction in her daughter's expanded opportunities; she can see her daughter's achievement as sweet compensation for the limited options of her own youth. Surely the first Chinese mothers who ˙re no longer forced to bind their daughter's feet must have re- ' to see their adult daughters striding about the countryside ˙d.

˙ite temptation for parents, not given to envy and ˙o give in to the primitive desire to have one's ˙uccessful, to have them make up for all past ˙ed. "I was poor, but my children are going to have everything." "I couldn't get an education, but my children will be doctors and lawyers." "They are never going to suffer like I did."

But parental designs to receive reparations for their own disappointments through their children's successful climb in the world should be checked. Common family experience, along with many a myth, reveals the folly of excessive parental ambitions. Driven parental agendas put onerous pressures upon children. Today many adult children in America suffer from the demand that they *must* be more successful and more fulfilled than their parents — they also have to be happy all the time.

Obviously it is better if parents of adults have just the right amount of push and family pride — not too much, not too little. Parents should be able to be happy if they are being outstripped by their wonderful progeny, but on the other hand they should not exert excessive demands that their adult children do much better or at least as well as themselves.

If parents are without too rigid an agenda, adult children can be liberated from intense anxieties over failure, or neurotic fears of success. They do not have to do better than their parents, but on the other hand they can stop worrying if they should overshadow father, mother, or both, by their greater accomplishments. Respecting the fact that adult children are unique individuals living in a unique moment in history, is the best way to go in family life. Confronting individuality is another inevitable challenge for parents of adult children.

Parents Need to Accept That Adult Children Have Become Who They Are through Their Own Choices and Chance Events

In middle-aged parenting when children are adults they are grown up and have already "turned out." The open future of the newborn and toddler has been narrowed. By the middle twenties, a young adult's life has already progressed into the opening scenes of its second act. The finger has written and moved on;

family time is as irreversible as any other. While many new developments in life are possible — in America we now live long enough to have time for third and fourth acts — *everything* is no longer possible.

By young adulthood an individual's own choices have interacted with different environmental pressures and chance events to produce a unique person with a specific character and personality. A parent has exercised influence, of course, but not full control. At this point in young adulthood a parent must come to terms with the grown-up individual that a child has become. The magic child of one's dreams has to give way to the present existing person who has developed in his or her own way. And since no character is without some flaw, a parent has to recognize that the most fair-haired child is imperfect and has limitations like the rest of the world. Parents have to accept their adult children's actual personalities rather than cherish illusions about who they could be, should be, or soon will be, once they get straightened out.

Jane Smiley in her fine novella *Ordinary Love* depicts a loving mother of grown children who muses, "I try to accept the mystery of my children, of the inexplicable ways they diverge from parental expectations, of how, however much you know or remember of them, they don't quite add up." And then she adds, "I have learned, over the last twenty years, to embrace the possible and not to mourn the rest." Many wise parents have learned the same lesson. Parents give up their grandiose expectations; it is enough to marvel at the mysterious separate identity of an adult child. I may have engendered this life and known this human being since birth, but now there is an adult who leads his or her life apart from mine.

Watching the progress of a child's growth from infancy to adulthood is an immersion course in the processes of unique human development, even if painful, uneven, and disappointing at times. Unfortunately, many American parents started out family life with misleading fantasies of omnipotence. These grandiose ideas included a belief that they as parents would shape their children's nature like clay and control their destiny. They planned to have children with all of their own good characteristics and none of their weaknesses. As one mother said, "I wanted my adult children to be just like me, only a lot better." Parents hope that they will have children who will carry on all of the parents' most cherished cultural ideals — without any of the pain and struggle that the parents had to endure in their own development.

Maybe romantic illusions of being an all-good, all-protecting parent producing a perfect child are necessary to help launch families. The reality of course is that the most loving and accomplished parents cannot control how their adult children turn out. Even in Plato's dialogues, more than two thousand years ago, one finds a puzzled discussion of how it can be the case that a virtuous man, providing his son with all the best tutoring, can not ensure that his adult child will also be morally virtuous. Why do good parents not automatically have good children? Or more optimistically, why do some rotten parents, or mediocre careless parents, produce saints and heroes?

Today we acknowledge that there are always factors beyond the control of a parent that can affect an adult child's character. There is the initial genetic throw, followed by random environmental effects; there are generational and peer social influences, but most important of all, a growing child exercises free will and chooses his or her own life path. A person is who he or she has chosen to become, and is not simply what a parent hath wrought.

When wise parents of today's adults talk about "letting go" of grown children, they are not talking about ceasing to care or ceasing to desire contact and communication or refusing love and mutual aid. They are talking about letting go of the magical blueprints that may have been lurking about in the parent-child relationship. They are also talking about accepting an adult child's need to have a separate life of their own.

Other parents may also talk more ominously about "giving up" — that is, relinquishing any hope that a child is ever going to change his or her life for the better. Every parent finally has to accept that this adult offspring is in control of his or her own life; no one can live for another person or be responsible for how that person turns out.

Parents should recognize that a family with grown children is a group of adults who in the course of decades may have turned out to be quite different from one another. The diversity of personalities and character in a family, whether marked or minimal, leads to another inevitable challenge for parents of adults.

Parents Need to Accept
the Diversity in a Family of Adults

In every family there are affinities and dissonances between different personalities within the family. Different temperaments, characteristics, and life-styles of family members mean that parents will have different reactions to different children, and the other way round. Siblings will differ from each other and have their own degrees of closeness or alienation among themselves. In a family some personalities are more attractive or easier for everyone to get along with and some individuals can be more prickly. Parents have to make the best of the existing cast of characters. If the "goodness of fit" between the personality of a parent and each adult child is equally wonderful, then well and good. If the siblings also get along well with each other, then ideal harmony reigns.

But sometimes the natural fit between parents and some of their grown children may be less than ideal. In many cases parents can admit privately in their own mind that they would never have freely chosen a particular adult child as a friend. As we all recognize, once we admit free will, genes, and chance, parents cannot control the fact that their adult children may not share their own temperaments, talents, interests, or values. A parent-child relationship may not be one of easy compatibility. Sometimes the personality or style developed by an adult child is one that a parent finds annoying.

Everyone has heard parents complain that some of their adult children are difficult to get along with — maybe they are too much like an unacceptable part of themselves, or too much like other family members with whom the parent has conflicts. At the same time a parent may feel particularly attuned to another adult child who is more naturally companionable. A parent would be drawn to this young adult even if he or she weren't a son or daughter. Occasionally an adult child's personality and gifts are so attractive that everyone in and out of the family will find them admirable and magnetic. The appearance of an all-around star who is successful and easy to get along with leaves a parent intensely grateful.

Acknowledging parent-child compatibility is no problem, but owning up to incompatibility is often avoided. Such reactions are denied because loving parents don't want to be unfair even in their thoughts and they don't want to hurt a child's feelings. In novels there is more latitude and a mother can be depicted admitting that her adult daughter "gets on my nerves." Or a disgruntled father can say, "I have a son who, though we are affectionate with each other, is no more my true son than if he breathed through gills. That is no gap between the generations, that is a gulf." This character sounds as though he believes the pessimistic observation that the different generations exist in order to disappoint each other.

No matter what gulfs of incompatibility may exist, the power of kinship ties arise from the fact that one is in an irreversible relationship with a person one did not choose. You select your spouse, but your parents and children are handed to you. Of course you are handed to them as well. The irreversibility of the family connection is beyond contract and choice. The given, involuntary nature of kinship has its negative and positive dimensions. We are all stuck, but we are stuck together. We are presented with the moral challenge of learning to get along with, and even grow to love, those relatives we never would have chosen as friends.

Many good parents will try especially hard to love and be attentive to a child with whom they are less compatible. Few democratic Americans could ever be at peace if they felt that they had unfairly favored one of their children over another, or loved one child less than the others. Not so an eccentric Oxford don in Nancy Mitford's comic novel, *Don't Tell Alfred*. Alfred, who has been called from Oxford to become the English ambassador to

Paris has a unique attitude to his four adult sons. When his wife is worrying whether she loved her more troublesome adult son David less than her other sons, Alfred reassures her, "One must see things realistically, my darling. You love him less because he is less lovable — it's as easy as that. . . . He has always been exactly the same . . . he was born so — . "

Alfred's insouciant belief that genetic determination rules family relationships and compatibilities is not particularly reassuring for parents who take a more rigorous view of environmental influences and their parental responsibilities. Yes, we can agree with Alfred that some children may be innately less attractive to a parent, and harder to like, but that doesn't resolve the moral problem. Ought not a good parent take more efforts and try harder with these more difficult personalities, not just give in to temperamental inclinations without putting up a fight?

One thinks here of the failure of easygoing, detached Mr. Bennet, in Jane Austen's *Pride and Prejudice.* He withdrew emotionally from the stupid members of his family (including, alas, his wife) and gave up on his parental duties. He maintained contact only with his favorites, his two intelligent, compatible daughters — with disastrous results for the rest of the family.

Most parents, however, are determined to be just. They do not want to be guilty of unfairness and they certainly do not want friction between siblings in the family although they may not be able to prevent it. Unfortunately, a perennial theme in families since Cain and Abel is the unpredictability of sibling interactions. Will it be love, hate, or indifference? Since Adam and Eve parents have had to negotiate their relationships with their adult children mindful of sibling rivalry. The more children in a family the more distinct personalities there are in constant interaction with each other and with their parents.

Siblings share 50 percent of their genes but they can end up very different or very alike. Developmental psychologists have tried to understand the subtle mix of environmental forces and individual characteristics that work toward sibling similarities and sibling differences. Spouses who are very different from each other offer different models for siblings to identify with, and if the family lives in an environment with many different outside exemplars, different siblings may choose to go different paths. We can think of the various brothers and sisters of recent presidents as a public example of sibling variation. Jimmy Carter's brother Billy and his two sisters were an example of the range of personalities possible in one middle-class American family, and one with stable rural roots. Other families who are dispersed or where harsher conditions prevail can produce even starker contrasts between children in the same family. A black college professor has written the sad history of the younger brother he left behind in the ghetto, while he escaped to college. The younger brother turned to drugs and crime and was eventually sent to prison. These parents had watched one child move up and out of the ghetto while the other succumbed to the dangers of the environment.

Parents who are committed to each of their children want all of them to flourish, and hope that in the process family harmony and a legacy of solidarity can be forged. An elderly father of five adult children reported how happy it made him that during the summer his children and their respective families had been visiting each other and enjoying themselves. He knows his own death is near; the mutual support his sons and daughters can give each other after he has gone gives him joy now.

But no matter how much parents try to prevent it, sometimes the relationships between siblings become strained or hostile. Brothers and sisters may become indifferent or estranged from one another, even though they maintain good relationships with their parents. Two sons refuse to speak or sisters never call one another. Parents of adult children can suffer a great deal when their children are incompatible, argue, or actually hurt one another. When two adult children quarrel it can be hell on their parents. Parents can empathetically feel the hurt of their wounded child and simultaneously be upset, angry, and/or ashamed at the behavior of the adult child who is inflicting the hurt.

One father and mother, for example, were disappointed and angry when Allan, one of their adult sons, refused to attend his brother Bob's wedding, despite being begged to do so. Even though Allan maintained that he was only adhering to his long-standing principles against marriage, his parents and his siblings thought his behavior adolescent and callous. It took years before this breach of family solidarity was mended.

Other parents report how painful it was when their two daughters had a fierce squabble over their grandmother's legacy of jewelry and furniture. Parents can be disheartened to see their supposedly grown-up children regress to childish fighting. Some research has shown that most parents in their wills divide their money and goods exactly evenly between siblings, in a final effort to forestall fighting over claims of favoritism. The parent as peacemaker among siblings is a role that a parent may never succeed in leaving behind completely.

But perhaps parents should stay out of their adult children's lives altogether, whether it be conflicts within the family or over any other matter? In addition to other indictments directed at today's parents, a new accusation has it that parents are emotionally "overinvolved." A specter is raised before parents that they may be "smothering," "suffocating," or (most horrible!) "overadequate." Overadequate parents apparently set such high standards of behavior for themselves that their children are burdened ever after with a shameful sense of their own inadequacy. But where for goodness sake is the line to be drawn between "adequate" and "overadequate"? Perhaps parents should cultivate complete social and emotional detachment from their adult children's concerns — adopting some form of benign neglect. In the next chapter I examine the ins and outs of different views of the parental role today.

As a bridge to these next questions we can return to the comic dilemmas of Alfred and his wife in the embassy in Paris. Alfred, in his rationalist way, does not believe in indulging in human emotions, or in ever asking his adult children any questions. But Alfred has other strict parental principles as well. These principles are described by his wife when David, their unkempt difficult son, an Oxford graduate, unexpectedly turns up at an embassy party with an unknown young woman and mysterious Chinese baby in tow:

"Alfred's reactions were not as immediately enthusiastic as mine. With him it is not so much a physical instinct as a matter of principle that makes him welcome the boys whatever the circumstances of their arrival. Our house is their home, their shelter from the stormy blast. If they are naked they must be clothed; if hungry, fed; if the police of five nations are hot on their heels they must be hidden. No questions must ever be asked." Without ever resorting to a direct question, Alfred and his concerned wife finally deduce that yes, their son is married to his shabby waif of a companion who is visibly pregnant. The young couple tell other dinner guests that they and baby Chang (whose is it?) are planning to walk to China in search of Truth. But in no time at all the mysterious baby gets dropped off with the parents in the embassy, while son and wife waft away following their guru.

One gets the distinct impression that Mitford's comic novel of parents beset by impossible adult children is, among other things, a deliberate spoof of the demands of modern parenthood. If the situation sounds farfetched I know of an American family of adult children who had a similar experience. Their son dropped in unexpectedly from Alaska for Thanksgiving accompanied by a young woman and her (not his) baby. The baby cried continually through a rather strained holiday week, but eventually all the visitors returned to the far north. Following Alfred's eccentric principles, these and other parents would end up giving their adult children shelter forever, with no questions asked. But once questions are permitted, the principles governing parental obligations may be somewhat revised — or at least turn out to be somewhat more complicated.

CHAPTER TWO

Out of the Nest:
Pushing, Nudging, Shoving?

What is there left for parents to do after the children have graduated from college? Haven't parents fulfilled their function if they have brought up their children and helped them get an education? Apparently not. An earlier understanding of parenthood may have thought college was the end, but today's parents find their role more complicated and prolonged. In the midst of shifting sands many parents want some bedrock on which to stand. What makes a good parent? Or even a good-enough parent?

In the last chapter I talked of inevitable conditions that all parents of adults should accept, such as the inexorable fact that the next generation will take over, the need to recognize that adult children have made choices already and become distinct individuals, and the need to accept the fact that a family of diverse adults may not all be equally compatible. But isn't there some more positive ideal or norm of good parenting that would work no matter what the challenges a parent could confront?

The Core of Good Parenting

An essential core of good parenting, in my view, remains continuous throughout early, middle, or late stages of parenthood. Good

29

parents are committed to their children, and the parental commitment consists of attentiveness, empathy, partiality, and the will to further the well-being of this particular son or daughter. As a parent, I am on my children's side; I celebrate all the good that comes their way and mourn their pain and setbacks. I will be intensely devoted to their well-being as long as we both live.

Obviously, this core commitment of a parent to a child will take different forms at different times in the life cycle and in different circumstances. Parental attention, empathy, and commitment can be played as minor or major themes. How a parent's preferential devotion is orchestrated will depend on what a child's welfare demands and what a parent can manage. It can range from the intense day and night nurturing of infancy, the initial "parental emergency," to the loving gaze of a fragile bedridden old parent upon the face of a middle-aged child.

In the all-out active phase from a child's birth to adolescence, parental commitment will include physical protection, nurturance, shelter, education and discipline. Parents will try to develop their child's capacities, while aiming to produce a socially acceptable adult fit for life with other people in and out of the family.

Parents of young children have an obligation to control and teach their children directly as well as influence them indirectly by being good examples in an environment that is as safe and stimulating as the parents can manage. The parental models and environment supplied produce children's first assumptions about the world. "Let us be merry and celebrate often," said one young parent. "We're creating our children's good old days." Moreover, parents are their children's first love objects and their first primary partners in activities ranging from peek-a-boo to the increasingly complex games of social life. Parents serve as the first appreciative audience that a child can command for new achievements. The parental audience for talking, writing, working, and so on, may be internalized and carried around in the head for life, so for the sake of a child's future self-confidence, it is important that parents be benign and encouraging.

The intense twenty-four-hour-a-day parental responsibility of the first years gradually changes as children grow up, first into adolescence and then into adulthood. Children have to move from being physically, psychologically, and emotionally dependent upon their parents to being independent adults. If young adults are going to get married, reproduce, make a living, and be citizens in the wider community they have to find new partners in life and move beyond the family circle. The eccentric example of Elizabeth Barrett Browning's nineteenth-century paterfamilias has to be an exception. Papa Browning forbade his adult sons and daughters from marrying, so to leave home they had to defy him, give up their inheritance and elope. His ideal of the family was a completely static one in which he reigned and the children obeyed.

Good parents who are dedicated to their children's welfare take as their imperative the task of encouraging movement toward a grown-up family of equally competent adults who can found homes of their own if they choose. One familiar version of this story has it that parents start out as benevolent despots, then turn into constitutional monarchs, move on to senators in a republic, and finally end up as fellow citizens in a democracy. This analogy from politics doesn't do justice to the continuing emotional bonds of parents and adult children, but it does describe the necessary shift toward equality of competence that parents and adult children have to manage. Unfortunately, the transitions can be bumpy in times of rapid social change and economic troubles. Parents today are facing new puzzles, challenges, and conflicts.

Problems and Challenges

In any gathering of middle-aged parents you can hear the same complaints. Adult children in their twenties and thirties remain in need of financial and emotional support, and many of them keep coming back home, again, and yet again, earning the name of "the boomerang generation."

Young adults come back home because in today's economy

they have lost their jobs, or have not been able to find a job, or have a job that pays so little that they cannot get enough money together to move into an apartment of their own. Or the apartment they could afford is in such a dangerous slum that parents are afraid to have them live there. Adult children return home to go to graduate school when a B.A. doesn't seem enough of a credential to get an entry-level job, or when they want to change careers. They come back when live-in relationships and marriages fail, sometimes, in the case of divorced daughters, accompanied by their children. They return home because of unforeseen crises and disasters — with a debilitating illness or after a devastating automobile accident.

It has become clear to one and all that many young adults are finding the entry into full maturity and self-sufficiency difficult. We read news stories of "the postponed generation," or "boomeranging," "adult returnees" making their "declarations of dependence." Cold statistics back up the general impressions that the new crop of adults are taking longer to get started in careers or to marry and found families of their own. More adults than in the past generation will never marry, and those who do, marry later and may remain childless. To be single or to be voluntarily childless are more acceptable choices than they were thirty years ago. (Single parenthood is also new, but I will discuss that in the chapter on changes in sex and reproduction.)

Young adults do a lot of floundering around and while they are "finding themselves" they depend upon their parents for economic and emotional support. It sometimes seems as though adolescence has been extended well into the third decade or even to forty. A recent novel was entitled, rather ominously, *A Girl of Forty*, and culture watchers talk of the Peter Pan syndrome afflicting men who remain eternal boys.

Without full-scale career commitments or family obligations many adult children appear to their parents as extremely immature for their age. Adult children who do not physically return to live at home may ask their parents for help with graduate school bills or with other financial expenses such as health care or initial down payments on housing. "Whatever happened to the idea of up and out?" complained one frustrated father as he reached for his checkbook once again.

Parents committed to their children's welfare are not sure what to do when adult children have trouble becoming financially and emotionally independent. Parents can be both surprised and anxious at these new developments. "Have I raised a deadbeat who can't make it?" "Is there something wrong with our family?" There are at least three parental responses to these new family challenges. Each of the different approaches depends upon a different assumption about what a family ought to be. One set of responses assumes the normalcy of the extended family household, another rejects family ties altogether, and a third continues to have as a goal cooperating, close, self-sufficient separate households for the different generations in the family. Those with the third goal have to adjust to the fact that in a "structurally declining economy," or hard times, this independence or interdependence of parents and children will take a lot more help from parents and many more years than it used to. These solutions are quite different.

The Multigenerational Extended Family Household

Parents facing new family emergencies and economic hard times can return to the way extended families have always operated: several generations of family members reside together and pool their resources for shared family goals. In traditional extended families, like those of many of today's Asian and Hispanic immigrants, parents expect their unmarried adult children to remain at home along with their married children and grandchildren. The multigeneration family pulls together to survive and to advance. Those who adopt this family style in response to present-day social changes can see themselves as returning to strategies that worked in their immigrant or rural past.

The extended family in which adult children, married and unmarried, reside and work with their parents and siblings, has been a mainstay for many people in America. The extended family is often found in rural living, and often reemerges during times of social strife or economic recessions and depressions.

In Alabama after the Civil War my great-great-grandfather Sion Jacob Perry's plantation household contained eight adults and fourteen children — grandparents, unmarried aunts and sisters, married sons with their wives and children. And this number had been lessened by one daughter's marriage and a son, a Methodist minister, who returned from the war, picked up his wife, children and handicapped brother (!) and went to Texas. The unmarried great-aunts were cared for on the homeplace until they died. In such a traditional pattern of family living it is often considered odd or unacceptable for a young adult to move out and live alone.

In a traditional family that lives and works together there are usually accepted forms of authority and family hierarchies that operate to maintain order. The father rules, or the grandfather rules, or the parents jointly rule — and everyone else recognizes this leadership in social and economic decision making. Traditional families do not run by democratic consensus with equal voting rights, or guarantees of individual liberties. Conformity to custom and the power of family authority is the price of solidarity and economic support. Certainly in traditional families the unmarried adult children do not consider it their due to have sex at home, or keep their own incomes to spend on cars and Club Med vacations!

Traditional patterns of extended family living can have advantages and satisfactions for parents, whether freely chosen or adopted out of economic necessity. As many families found in the last great depression in the 1930s, coping with external pressure strengthens family bonds. As a parent, you don't lose touch with your adult children and grandchildren when they live with you. Children in an extended family have many adults who love and care for them; there are many models of adulthood around and if there is a divorce or a death, the children will be nurtured. Aging parents get help and support at home. The nest never empties. It won't be a trauma if you have to live with your children when you are old, because you're already there. The mix of generations in a full house can be a permanent condition of life, not just a twenty-year episode. Parents turn into grandparents without much of a change in family composition or responsibilities.

The disadvantages of returning to a traditional extended family life can also be numerous. People left extended families and chose to live in private nuclear families because life in common breeds conflicts as well as affection. Traditional multigenerational families produce their own pressures on everyone concerned. Extended families living together can be particularly hard on married couples who have less privacy and are caught in multiple allegiances to spouse, parents, children, and siblings. For modern American families it is never an easy matter to revise individualistic expectations; indeed, autonomy, privacy, and independence, if not overdone, are valued goods that enhance personal life. But overdoing the culture's emphasis upon individualistic autonomy is the basis of another response to the problems adult children may present.

Acclaiming Individual Autonomy and Detachment from the Family

A minority response to new pressures from adult children can be found in those new-age parents who reject obligations to help adult children who may be floundering. These individualists do not accept parental commitment as permanent and champion an afamilial or post-child-rearing style of life. Many Americans enthusiastically endorse ideals of freedom and autonomy in the service of personal fulfillment. If free choice and individual self-fulfillment are at the top of a person's value hierarchy then family ties and kinship obligations will be discounted. Converts to the cult of self-fulfillment and autonomy are not all young. Some middle-aged parents seem to lead the way in family dissolution citing as maxims, "Now it's my turn," and "I owe it to myself."

In one family I know, the father divorced the mother and more or less abandoned their five children. The mother in her turn sold up and moved to the West Coast to start a new life in a tiny apartment. The adult children were now on their own, scattered over the country without a family center or permanently engaged parent. Neither mother or father were interested in maintaining their family ties, for in their eyes the years together were a period of unhappy domesticity that they wished to leave behind.

Parents today can remain in good health and at mid-life look forward to many more decades of life; it is possible for them to start new careers, new marriages and other new experiments in living. Divorced middle-aged mothers can go back to graduate school or join communes, fathers can marry again and start new families or go to live on a sailboat the year round. There are powerful social currents in America that glorify the protean self, the ideal of an ever-changing, constantly renewing movement of the self through new identities. If I am now a new and different person, how can I be bound by claims from the past? The past is irrelevant. An adult child from an old marriage may not fit into a parent's present quest for self-fulfillment.

Another family-damaging ideological current in our society is the view that all moral obligations can be reduced to those contracts made with informed consent. Contracted obligations are only binding as long as both parties consent to the relationship. If the parent-child "contract" is viewed as extending until a child is an adult, then after age eighteen or twenty-one a parent is free and no longer bound. Of course at the other end of life, an adult child does not owe an old parent anything either. Whoever gave informed consent to be born the child of one's parents? In most jurisdictions there is no personal legal responsibility for one's old parents, just as there is no parental legal obligation for an adult child. Individual free choice rules. You don't even have to obtain a divorce to sever the adult parent-child relationship.

Sometimes the individual's endorsement of reversible, provisional commitments is clothed in spiritually toned psychobabble. Individuals are described as on a lonely journey-quest; each of us is ultimately alone in the existential quest for meaning and the inner self, "I am not put here to fulfill your expectations, you are not put here to fulfill mine," and so on. In this revisionist view of family life, parents are not abandoning their core parental commitment when they emotionally detach themselves from their adult children, but are helping their children to discover that each of us must make our own way. An affluent parent, or couple, can emotionally sign off, retire to a plush condominium in Arizona and send an occasional postcard. The upshot of individualism, contract morality, and new-age thought is that many parents are not available for any form of support for young adults. Parents refuse to become involved; when the children come around they won't be home.

Obviously, in a book entitled *Parents Forever*, I am not going to endorse an afamilial atomistic approach that abandons the bonds of kinship in the name of autonomy. But then neither do most Americans, who regularly put "their family" at the head of the list, when asked what matters most to them in life. But does putting family first mean that you must then embrace the traditional multigenerational extended family household, if and when difficulties with adult children arise? While this traditional way of coping may suit some parents and adult children, it can't be an ideal solution for everybody. Surely there is something to be said for a middle way.

Working toward Separate Households
in a Cooperative Family Network

A third way of coping with new challenges presented by adult children is the preferred American middle ground between the clan and individualism. Most parents will recognize the irreversible bonding and parental commitments of the extended family without giving up the privacy of separate self-sufficient households. I too subscribe to an ideal vision of the adult family in which mutual help, cooperation, and emotional closeness are always available, and in emergencies, you can move in together. But the generations do not aim to live together on a permanent basis. Adult children should be welcome to come home or stay home as a *temporary* measure; but returning to dependency in the family is seen as a means to achieving eventual independence or interdependence. Parents should be willing to serve as emergency backups and supplementary supporters, or even as ports of call for occasional rest and recuperation, but permanent common residence or dependency will be avoided if possible.

In this scenario parents will have their own private household near their adult children's own private households. Both households will be self-sufficient although frequently exchanging goods and services. The family members will help each other when needed and enjoy a great deal of visiting back and forth.

Like many parents of adult children I complain that I never see my adult children enough, and often miss them. Yet I wouldn't want us all to live together again permanently. Vacationing together, weekend visits and family celebrations of the holidays are enough — if we can have brief visits and frequent phone calls in between. I would like to live around the block from my adult children, but not in the same house, apartment, or two-family duplex where there was no visual privacy. Why not?

Part of my motivation is altruistic. I think it is better for adult children to live alone and learn to be socially self-sufficient, forging their own new ties with others. After all parents are going to die and adult children must have social skills, friendships, family bonds, and community commitments of their own. Even a handicapped or impaired adult child may be better off if he or she is well-established in a sheltered community away from home; parents cannot take care of him or her forever — and neither can the siblings.

When adult children live at home with their parents there is a temptation to sink back into the status of a child. (People report themselves regressing to old patterns of behavior the minute they cross their parents' doorstep.) It is also harder to feel the need to marry if a young adult is emotionally ensconced in the bosom of a large compatible family. Why venture forth to risky commitments, especially since in today's world it is easy to get sex on the side? Once married, young couples establishing a marriage and their own family can benefit from privacy in which to fight, deepen their intimacy, and create their own family culture and circle of friends. Better still, living together on their own neutral turf, neither spouse has to live as an in-law with their mate's family.

Living separately, parents and their adult children can have diverse friends and engage in activities beyond those of the family circle. It is rare indeed for everyone in the family to have the same tastes, values, or convictions, starting with music and ending with religious and political values. What you don't see or hear doesn't have to be explained or justified. Radical activist parents with more conservative children won't need to defend their political activities — or vise versa. Both generations may be living full professional lives with many different social and community obligations. These interests can flourish better in private living space without a family audience. Who wants to feel obligated to include the whole family every time you have a party?

Many parents, along with many of their adult children, choose privacy. Parents who are still married may want to live alone, but so can a divorced or widowed single parent. Middle-aged couples can enjoy and deepen their marital relationship when they are finally free of competing distractions and responsibilities. Alone at last! If a couple has stayed married for decades, through all the ups and downs of childbearing, and valiantly managed to remain friends and lovers, they can now delight in having more time for each other. (I know people stay married out of habit, or spite, but these apathetic or mutually tormenting marriages seem rarer in a day of easy divorce.)

In companionable long-term marriages a couple living alone can travel together, hike together, play tennis together, and enjoy their own September Song as the days dwindle down to a precious few. The everpresent threat of cancer, heart attacks, and Alzheimer's disease make one seize the day. Older couples report joy in their newfound freedom. When you live without family around if you don't want to cook, you don't. You no longer have to set a good example for anyone. Many parents who are long married, along with parents who are single, can relish their middle-age peace and solitude.

Over and over I have heard caring, committed parents of adult children say, "I love it when the kids come home. It's wonderful.

But it's also great when they leave!" Of course, this is a reaction to visits from adult children who live elsewhere. Admittedly, when adult children are living at home a routine evolves that relieves everyone of the pressures of being on holiday. As we all know, having fun can take twice as much out of you as working. Joy-filled events can be as exhausting as times of disaster. Any parent who has celebrated a happy family wedding will agree that it takes almost as many weeks to recover as if one had undergone major surgery.

Being with other people takes social energy, no matter how much one loves them or how happy they make you. I don't think it is selfish to cherish solitude if you have done your generative bit and now find that you are an inward introspective sort of person. I like to be alone, I'm never bored, and find it easy to read silently and write for hours at a time. I am not particularly domestic or social in my interests. While I welcome my family, friends, and my students, I also cherish a more contemplative life during those semesters when I don't teach.

When I am teaching, writing, and lecturing I live the kind of hectic schedule that many beleaguered workers do. Then I need even more private time alone at home to put myself back together. As one busy professional mother of adult children put it, "I was more tolerant of sharing my territory when I was younger, but now if I don't have time to myself I feel like I am dissolving, and there is no self left." I agree. If tomorrow I had to go back to living in an active extended family with my adult children, I'm sure that I could cope and even be very happy, but I prefer less companionship on a daily live-in basis. Even residing with my most compatible offspring would be something of a strain and living with those who are very different in temperament, habits, and interests would be uphill work indeed.

For those parents whose family goal is to live in different private households within a cooperative family network the question then becomes a matter of how best to encourage adult children to independence while keeping family bonds strong.

Helping Adult Children to Mature Independence

Parents have a delicate task when it comes to helping adult children to self-sufficiency and maturity. How can you help people without making them, through your intervention, more dependent? Being a passive recipient of aid can be diminishing. Individuals grow independent and self-sufficient by actively doing things for themselves, on their own. They learn to be strong as they engage in struggle. It isn't easy to help others to help themselves in or out of the family.

Certainly you don't give fish to the hungry without trying to teach them how to fish. But even the fishing lessons and supportive supervision, with backup provisions when the fish don't bite, may be counterproductive. At some point you have to leave the new fisherpersons alone to get on with it. Many adult children throughout history have been stunted and handicapped by too much parental help, given in the wrong way, for too long a time.

Parents have to think about the immediate and long-term effect of any help, be it money, presents, or room and board at home. Alfred's principles of parenthood, described in the last chapter, are not discriminating enough. The lifelong parental habit of nurturing and automatically giving has to become more self-conscious. Will this help I give further this young adult's growing-up process? If the helping hand is extended with the understanding that it is temporary and given as a boost toward eventual self-sufficiency, it can be a positive thing. Parents can be nurturing while simultaneously nudging the fledglings along on the bumpy path to solo flights.

As one mother put it, "I think they almost let you know when they are ready to have you push them out." This mother, a widow, took the initiative, found one of her sons an apartment and insisted that he move out. Her other children did not have the same problem moving on and away from home. Other parents have reported that it took several attempts and leave-takings before a young adult actually made it on their own in a new living situation. One family noticed that if a leave-taking had been stormy and angry, the child would come back. Final separation would only "take," when the parent-child relationship was in better shape. It was almost as though, in order to become a believable move to independence, a dreadful stormy scene would have to be rewritten with a better script.

Help given for onetime, unusual emergencies does not usually endanger the goal of eventual independence and maturity. An illness, an accident, sudden unemployment, a new baby, a divorce, efforts to buy a house — all of these are singular needs that have always elicited help from parents. The family has always served as a shield between the individual and disaster, as well as a source of supplementary economic help. The idea of nineteenth-century marriage settlements among the well-to-do, was to insure that the next generation would be financially secure. One-time provisions of aid need not become a dependent habit, and can rescue young adults from disaster or help them on their way. Parents have always used their discretionary income to foster the start-up of the next generation.

Of course, parents who are prudent will have to think about themselves and their own short and long-term prospects. If giving help to adult children is a real burden and endangers parental self-sufficiency then it is almost surely the wrong choice to make. Having impoverished elderly parents would be an unenviable future outcome for both the parents and their adult children. Parents may live to be a hundred, sometimes outliving their children, and so they have to be prepared to finance their own old age. The help that parents can offer in the present should not be too costly a sacrifice.

But most middle-class, fairly affluent parents are not in danger of falling into poverty through financial aid to their adult children. Many well-to-do parents cannot decide the question of whether to help or not by pleading their own financial needs. The more frequent situation is that parents have enough money to live in a more than comfortable style in the present, but they do not have enough money to support their children financially for their lifetime. They are only temporarily and superficially rich! Unlike the really rich, or aristocrats of another day, middle-class parents have earned enough money to live well, but do not have enough capital to provide incomes or trust funds for their children to depend upon. Therefore it is vital that adult children learn to fend for themselves. With this in mind, parents should not endanger their adult children's commitment to the work ethic by encouraging dependency.

The situation is made more complex by the fact that this generation of aging adults may be the last generation to have made more money and done better than their own parents. Today, as we have all been depressed to hear, parents and their adult children have to face the possibility of the next generation's downward mobility. A new generation of adult children may not be able to equal, or economically outstrip, their parents as a matter of course. The social and economic quality of life for many middle-class adults may be declining. Economists have ominously described the poor prospects of the coming generation, by calling them a generation "born to pay." Over the last decades real income has been declining (except among the most affluent) unemployment is rising and house prices have skyrocketed.

Parents can worry, "Will my children ever be able to buy a house?" In many a suburb or desirable section of the country, the inflation in real estate values guarantees that few adult children could ever afford to buy the house they grew up in — unless they happen to be a dual-income married couple composed of two physicians, two advertising executives, or a CPA married to a lawyer. These are the occupations of the young couples who were able to buy the houses up for sale on the street in the New York suburb where we used to live. Typically, the house we paid $72,000 for, sold fifteen years later for $450,000. A modest one bedroom condominium in this town now sells for $95,000. In the sixties our first house in this town cost $23,000, which with a $2,300 down payment we could afford to carry on my husband's salary of $9,000. I stayed home with three small children and we had more babies; we were poorer than shabby genteel, but it was a possible life.

Adult children can envy their parent's generation. As one young man who was no slouch in his journalistic achievements said to me, "My father owned a home in the suburbs, supported his wife and four children, but at thirty-eight I am still single and struggling to make ends meet." Of course there are the high-salaried young professionals who can buy Jaguars and houses, but there are not as many out there as the media hype of the eighties might have led one to believe. Parents whose children are not superaffluent may be sad to see how much less their adult children have been able to achieve compared to their own generation's opportunities at a comparable age.

When parents recognize that times have changed they begin to adjust their expectations and their willingness to help their children. So houses now cost six times as much as they once did, but real wages have not gone up. So an M.A. gets you what a high-school diploma once did. And having one baby costs more than having five babies a generation ago. Understanding the prevailing conditions in the society convinces parents of the need to help their adult children longer, with more financial support, than their own parents either could have, or would have. Parents can see themselves as a countervailing force against the greater obstacles young adults now encounter on the road to self-sufficiency. The whole process may be slower and try the patience of the whole family.

But at the same time parents who have the goal of mature independence for their children, don't want to disable their adult children by giving too much help. And they also don't want to be exploited or manipulated. Parents should resist helping adult children who think themselves automatically entitled to an upscale standard of living it took their parents a lifetime of hard work to achieve. Expectations and entitlements in youthful lifestyles seem to have escalated along with real estate values — and to be an equally unfortunate development. There may be heated generational differences of opinion about what constitutes a necessity of life and what is a desirable luxury. Moreover, most parents are willing to help their adult children when there is a real need, if and only if, the adult children are working hard for reasonable goals. If the adult child is presently living in a responsible adult way, that is proof of good intentions for the future.

On the other hand, why should playboys of the western world receive parental subsidies?

If a healthy adult child is not working and not making efforts to become independent, why should parents who have worked hard themselves endlessly provide shelter or send money? When adult children freeload or take advantage of their parents, parents have to demand a change in the family structure. If adult children have come home, either permanently or temporarily, they have to accept responsibility for maintaining the household. Those adults taking up family life in common have to accept a change in the ground rules; what was fitting for a nuclear family with small children is no longer appropriate for a house full of adults.

Parents in nuclear families with small children make many sacrifices in order to launch their children into independent adult self-sufficiency. But this pattern of one-way investment ought to be adjusted if the lift-off doesn't take place. When everyone in the family is still at ground zero then the child-centeredness of an earlier stage of family life is inappropriate.

When adult children come home to live they should come as grown-ups. Everyone has seen families where the adult children are catered to and indulged as though they were still youngsters. More young men than young women, apparently, live at home and depend upon their mothers to cook for them and do their laundry. Parents can feel exploited if adult children living at home do not pay a fair share of the expenses or do not do household chores. Conflict escalates if the young adults do not abide by the family's established moral standards in regard to drink, drugs, or sex.

Parents should assert their authority and should make firm demands that their own standards be met in the home. Parents do not assert their claims to authority solely on the grounds of age, property rights or because they have more money, but because it is morally right that whoever has founded a family and put in years of committed effort gets to set the rules. The founders of the household who have worked to establish it and keep it going possess sweat equity and founders' rights.

Ironically, many good parents facing returning adult children are handicapped by their own past efforts at good childrearing. What was adaptive and successful in an earlier stage of childbearing no longer is appropriate. When children are small, responsible parents should put the children's needs first. If they are Americans, most parents will also try to meet the unique individual needs of each child in order to further that particular child's optimal development. But the individualistic ideal of meeting the unique needs of each and every child, makes it difficult to shift gears in an adult family and demand effort for the common good. Many parents find themselves engaged in conflicts with their adult children that they were not prepared to face.

Conflict

As all family survivors know, conflict between parents and grown children comes in all degrees of seriousness, and about all sorts of different issues. I will discuss conflict many times in the course of this book. There are always superficial disagreements that are quickly resolved either because the occasion passes or the conflict is settled by mutual agreement. Some parent-child conflict is almost inevitable between two people if both are alive, awake, and openly communicating with one another. Intimacy uncovers disagreements, and different points of view collide. Contesting family differences can prove stimulating and interesting, if there is not too much conflict over too many serious issues — and if parents and children manage not to harm each other.

Unfortunately in some families conflict escalates and estrangements between parents and adult children occur. Almost all communication is severed. I know several sets of good parents, judged by any standard, who have been repudiated by one of their adult children for obscure and ambiguous reasons that neither the parents nor anyone else can fathom. (And these are not cases of the adult child's joining a cult.) It seems as though the adult child has to manufacture hostility and continues to project some personal demon or inner struggle upon his inoffensive parents. This alienation causes the parents pain and suffering, as repeated efforts to restore the relationship fail.

I also know parents who in response to their adult child's criminal drug use were the ones who insisted on breaking off contact. They felt they had to ensure their own safety and that of the rest of the family. If everything in the family home is going to be stolen to buy drugs, and physical violence is threatened or erupts, parents declare the family home off limits. Calling the police to have one's child taken away has got to be the nadir of parenthood. Many parents of drug addicts or mentally ill adults have had to do this. But no matter who institutes the break, or for what reason, the lost son or absent daughter fractures the family circle.

Wallace Stegner, in one of his fine novels, has a disappointed father reflect on the break between himself and his adult son, Curt. Curt had bitterly rejected his father's work ethic and chosen to live as a surfing bum on a California beach. Unfortunately, Curt dies in a surfing accident in his pursuit of the eternal present, closing the door on any future reconciliation. Decades later the father still suffers: "Curt's repudiations let the air out of my confidence that I know what my job, my principles, my vote, my admirations, my friends, and my marriage are all about.... In rejecting me he destroyed my compass, he pulled my plug, he drained me. He was the continuity my life and effort were spent to establish."

Parents invest so much in their children that disappointments and serious conflicts can cast them into depression. There is enough pain floating around in so many families that tactful souls hesitate to ask, "What are your children doing?" Some preliminary probing may be in order to see if the topic of adult children is one to avoid. Yet many other parents may be bursting with pride at their progeny's achievements. As one father remarked, "Other people's children all seem to be Rhodes scholars or neurology residents." The most serious disagreement reported in

...nilies is a fight a mother reported over whether her daughter should go to the prestigious medical school where she was accepted rather than enrolling in the second-rate psychology graduate program the mother felt would be wrong for her. Parents with such high-level "problems" can hardly envision the crises and conflicts that other parents face.

Conflicts between parents and their adult children may sometimes demand immediate parental action. Grim moments in family life arise when parents feel that they must make a stand. Such confrontations often occur when an adult is still dependent upon parental financial support — or still living at home. Parents who rightly demand that in their own home their own moral standards of acceptable behavior be observed may find their guidelines constantly ignored. When an adult child refuses to work, go to school, seek therapy, or conform to family standards of conduct, parents can feel mounting anger and anxiety. Why is this young adult collapsing back into this childlike dependency and self-destructive rebellious behavior? Should I demand that he leave the house?

Parents can feel paralyzed and helpless. Habits of going the second mile and generations of a family's heritage of loyalty and commitment to one's kin make the thought of ousting one's own flesh and blood a hard step to take. If in the turmoil a mother and father disagree about what to do, a stalemate can ensue. Often parents swing back and forth between making demands and setting rules for better behavior, and when that fails, backing down and continuing to provide support.

Parents faced with adult children who are engaging in seriously troubled and offensive behavior have a problem in discerning what is happening. Is this adult child seriously neurotic, chemically addicted, or somehow mentally impaired? Or is this a person capable of self-sufficiency but refusing to make the effort? When one determines the child is unimpaired and is capable of acting in a responsible grown-up way, it is time to act. Two concepts which are almost clichés by now can help: one is "enabling" and the other, "toughlove."

Enabling and Toughlove

In America we have learned about "enabling" from the spread of alcohol and drug-addiction treatment programs. Ideas found in AA and AlAnon and other twelve-step programs have permeated the rest of society. Enablers are defined as those persons who by their inappropriate help make it possible for addicted persons to drink, take drugs, or commit violence without having to bear the consequences of their destructive behavior. Enabling activities may be direct, such as procuring a drug, providing the money or setting up the opportunity for the drug use, or indirect, such as providing cover-ups — making excuses to employers, or doing the other person's job in his or her stead. In other words enablers help a person to act in an irresponsible way and get away with it.

The advice given to all enablers is to withdraw the direct or indirect support that is making the other person's destructive behavior possible. Any aid that helps a person to continue to self-destruct or harm others should no longer be provided. Parents of course are natural enablers because at an early stage of childhood benign enabling is the whole point of protective parental nurturing. But with adult children, inappropriate helping should be stopped. If you are truly committed to the welfare of another adult you have to refuse to keep protecting and cooperating with that person's destructive way of life. The assumption is that persons on an irresponsible course will not change until they have to pay the costs and penalties of their wrongdoing. They may have to hit bottom in order to realize that they should seek help and begin to change.

Parents caught in a serious conflict with a rebellious dependent young adult can finally refuse to support unacceptable behavior. As a last resort, parents can ask their child to leave the house and cut off funds. One mother and father who finally demanded that their adult son leave the house reported that it was the hardest thing that they had ever done. But they felt it was the only thing they could do to help stop their son's self-destructive life of drinking and dissipated behavior. They recognized they were facilitating his way of life when they let him live, eat, and sleep the day away at home. When their adult son refused to work full-time, refused to go to school, or go to therapy, his parents refused to allow him to stay at home.

This mother said that she suffered terribly, fearing that her son might come to harm living on the streets. But at the same time she could no longer support her stubborn, passive aggressive son as he rotted away in his room. Something needed to be done and refusing to cooperate was the parent's only option. In this case the son did survive; he wore out his welcome with his peers and finally had to go to work. Eventually he returned to school and went for therapy. His parents, who were well-to-do, agreed to pay for schooling and therapy, but would do so only if he worked to help himself. Every move he took that displayed disciplined effort they would match, but only if he carried through step by step. Eventually this intelligent young man struggled through college, and went on to receive his master's degree from an Ivy League school. His gradual progress to self-esteem and maturity reestablished the rapport with his parents, and with himself. All the parental anxiety and pain he caused is now forgiven, if not forgotten.

Making parental demands and refusing to support a child who is not acting in an acceptable way has been given the name of *toughlove*. A movement of therapists and self-help groups has developed to support parents who have been exploited or manipulated by their adult children. When parents are unable to cope they need help. The point of toughlove, as with enabling, is to help parents see that love does not mean helping another to be irresponsible, self-destructive, and bully others. If parents let themselves be unfairly victimized, then they are encouraging their child to be oppressive and unprincipled with others. Parents have to demand mature responsible behavior even if they have to cut off contact until their children change. Parents still can be committed to their children's welfare, but the permissiveness and unconditional approval that is appropriate for an infant is not appropriate for an adult.

Yet parents will suffer whatever happens. Helplessly watching a beloved child make self-destructive choices can produce intense bouts of despair. Parents are empathetically and emotionally involved, but have no control over events. All they can do is state their position, and refuse to aid and abet behavior by withdrawing support. A decision to refuse help is so traumatic for most caring parents that they would do well to get some outside support. Parents identify so much with their children and have so much at stake that it may be difficult for them to see the objective reality of a situation.

Parents may tend to be either too soft and permissive or, at the other extreme, too angry and overcontrolling. (It is not unknown for very rigid or hostile parents to misuse and abuse the idea of toughlove.) Other trusted persons — wise friends, therapists, pastors — can help reach a balanced perspective. There is no more painful dilemma of parenthood than this: Am I failing in charity and my parental commitment by refusing to help my child, or am I failing in charity and my parental obligation by helping inappropriately? These are exercises in discernment and prudence that can never be taken lightly; whatever the decision it will be an irreversible part in the family story.

One other crucial truth stressed in the idea of toughlove and enabling, which is a theme woven through this book, is the affirmation of free will; adults, be they parents or children, are free to choose between different options that life presents. Unless they are mentally impaired, individuals can choose to follow moral promptings and recognized moral obligations, or they can turn away and act against what they know to be right. Parents have to recognize that adult children are making their own choices, just as they themselves are.

Overidentification with children can be damaging to both parent and child. Sweetly arrogant Lady Marchemaine, the mother-martyr of Evelyn Waugh's *Brideshead Revisited*, makes an outrageous if familiar parental claim when she sighs, "Ah my dear, any failure of my children is my failure." Why, for goodness sake? Are there not two separate individuals involved? The omnipotent obtuseness of this claim can be uncovered by asking the Lady Marchemaines and other guilt-ridden parents of the world whether they blame all their own failings on *their* parents? And theirs on theirs, and so on? Certainly not, although Lady Marchemaine probably took upon herself blame for the sins of the previous and the next generation, as well as for those of her poor husband.

If an adult son or daughter cannot even lay claim to his or her own guilt then they have to keep upping the ante of infraction (like Sebastian) and they are robbed of taking any pride in being responsible for their own achievements.

It is well to remember that in the Biblical story of the prodigal son the father's joy took place *after* the prodigal son had repented of his ways, decided to change his life, and to come home and ask forgiveness. Would this most loving of fathers have kept sending money to the far country to finance his son's dissipation with harlots? No, not likely. It may have been necessary for this weak and wrongheaded son to end up tending pigs on an empty stomach before he could confront his own behavior more clearly — and begin to appreciate his father's way of life.

But the story of the prodigal son, with its real-life counterparts — resentful elder siblings are always with us too — can give parents hope during times of estrangement. Young adults do turn their lives around. Individuals can change. As time passes adult children — and their parents — can develop understandings of each other that lead to more perfect unions. Conflicts and hurts are healed. As one middle-aged mother said, reflecting on our longer life expectancies, "Now there are more years left for everyone to say I'm sorry." Having another extended round, another act in the drama can be a blessing. Reconciliation is possible.

CHAPTER THREE

Can We Be Friends?
The Art of Talking to Adult Children

When a mother I know says that her adult daughter is her best friend, some observers might dismiss her claim. But I argue that it is possible, even probable, for parents and their adult children to be good friends, if one proviso is made. While parents and children can be friends, they will always be "something more" as well.

In a parent-child friendship "the something more" comes from the fact that the emotional stakes are higher within the family than outside it. After all, parents can have many friends but only one relationship with a child. As the old joke goes, "Friends you have by the dozen, mothers come one to a customer." Friends may come and go, but if there is a break with a son or daughter the pain will last.

A father in Christopher Tilghman's story "A Father's Place" reflects on how much more important his son is to him than any of his other close friends, past or present. Dan the father fears losing his son Nick's affection. A crisis has arisen because Nick has brought home a dreadful girlfriend, Patty Keith, who browbeats Nick and is hostile to the rest of the family. Dan cannot abide her, but is worried about Nick's reaction if he should speak up. Suppose he alienates Nick? "In the end, thought Dan, being Nick's father didn't mean he and his son couldn't grow apart; didn't

53

mean a biological accident gave him any power over the situation. It only meant that it would hurt more. He could not imagine grieving over friends he once loved with all his heart and now never saw.... But Nick — even if he never spoke to him again, even if this Patty Keith took him away to some isolation of spirit, Dan would know where he was and feel the pain." An estranged son or daughter stays lodged in the heart.

Those who argue that parents and children can't really be friends bring as evidence the fact that the parent-child relationship is by nature, unique, complex, and emotionally intense; its weight will sink efforts to be friends. Can any parent or child ever escape the uniqueness of the bond, or achieve the freedom and equality necessary for friendship? Won't the psychological residues of childhood linger forever and get in the way? If parents exercised authoritative parental leadership when a child was small, can they now change?

But these objections overemphasize the inflexibility of parent-child relationships. As children grow into adults there is constant flux in a family. As many a parent has lamented, "Every time we get adjusted to some stage of our child's development, something new has happened." Parents of adults have already had years of gradually moving from one kind of parenting to another. As the years go by, parental authority and control ordinarily metamorphizes into an advisory relationship more like that of counselor, mentor, or consultant.

Counselors, mentors, and consultants can be friends and equals with the adults they guide. An advisory relationship is not adversarial and can be a two-way street, depending upon what's at issue and who needs advice about what. As children increase in maturity, they can become equal to their parents in many ways, and may supersede them in others. Some children by their innate intelligence, temperament, and personality, grow up so fast that they seem to have been born responsible and worldly wise. But in any event, persons don't have to be the same age or possess identical powers to be good friends.

Perhaps part of the argument depends on one's idea of what a friend is. As the dictionary defines it, a friend is "a person attached to another by feelings of affection or personal regard; a person who gives assistance, a supporter." What really counts in friendship is that two persons feel affection and regard. Good friends also tend to share values, have overlapping interests, and appreciate each other's sense of humor. (Playfulness is very high on my list of necessary requirements.) In friendship there is a deep affectionate interest in the other as a particular individual; we are interested in our friends for themselves, and not only because they stimulate us or make us feel happy. Friends are valued because they are who they are. As friends and fellow sojourners we are on each other's side, supporting each other in sorrow and strife and rejoicing together in good times. But this is what parenting an adult is all about. The core parental role, never outgrown, is attentiveness, empathy, partiality, and commitment to your child's welfare. This is nothing if not a form of intense, supercharged friendship.

The voltage comes from the fact that a friendship with adult children is powered by additional kinship commitments. Family ties magnetize the parent-child relationship. In addition to affection and attentive interest, friends in the family share their common roots. Inevitably, every family will have a history that includes turbulence and pain, but overall it is possible to have good will and good times predominate.

When parents and their adult children are friends they share all the present and future concerns that other friends share, along with their shared biography. Their conversation can include, "Remember when . . . ?" reminiscence as the mosaic of common memory begins to be filled in, chewed over, amended. It is a process much like those complex films and epic novels that tell a story from the different characters' divergent points of view. Middle-aged parents and their adult children looking back on some incident can take up the challenge of describing their own viewpoint *then*, along with their viewpoint *now*, capped off with the tale of their progress from then to now, and what this may, or may not, reveal about themselves, the times, and life in general. Every conversation adds to the ongoing stream, as past, present, and future reflections get interwoven.

When I now, at fifty-eight, remember myself as a busy young mother, I see a young woman in her twenties who was younger than my youngest child is today. The struggles and passions of that earlier time are now seen through the reverse end of the telescope. From this distance I can see my husband and myself as two earnest young things, babies raising babies. The changed perspective engenders calm detachment as painful past incidents are reduced to details in the crowded frieze of events still to come. A look at the moving picture of all the years also lets large themes and emerging patterns stand out more clearly. As another mother remarked when discussing her long-ago conflicts with her children and young husband, "Well, you know, it was rough because we were all growing up together."

Another revelation that comes to middle-aged parents looking even further back is the realization that when they first knew their own parents, those glamorous godlike figures were themselves in their twenties and thirties — also younger than one's adult children are now. "Was my father only thirty-four when we lived in the country and he was raising us by himself?" "Was my stepmother only twenty-eight when she took on my father and my sister and me as a ready-made family?" Zounds! Mid-life retrospectives reduce the status of "adult," and "grown-up," to a relativized category.

Family memories and imaginative recreations of the decades reassure us of the continuity of the passing generations. Stories of earlier generations are recalled and handed down. Family ties are knit together through reworking the common narrative and distinctive family theme. Emotions are engaged because this particular set of characters, and no other, is the permanent cast of your epic novel, *The Brothers Karamozov* rewritten. As the plot winds down these actors will people future episodes — including the final scenes.

Milestones in the family are observed, from marriages to births to graduations to anniversaries to funerals; celebrations are interspersed with rites of mourning. As psychologists now attest, familiarity with faces can produce unconscious preferences and liking. We seem to be a species predisposed to be attached to those known and familiar; the near tend to become dear. Friendships and affection naturally flourish between family members who have shared hours and hours of time and talk. Many, many parents and adult children claim that not only do they dutifully value each other, but that they are good friends as well. If the genius of human culture is that it makes us want to do what we must do in order to survive, then the invention of the family is culture's masterpiece. We want to form families and live with them; we enjoy reciprocal exchanges of food and other resources; we become friends with those with whom we share genes and strive to have them flourish.

This is not to say that today's parents and children who are friends will always tell each other everything. But who tells any friend everything? Friendships of all kinds have reserved topics that are off limits. A sense of boundaries and privacy is valued. Tactfulness and a sense of what is appropriate means that in most families sexual intimacies won't be described, and those things that may be hurtful to a family member will not be talked about. Few intimate friendships will be totally open; they do not have to be completely transparent in order to be highly satisfying.

Is my picture of parents and children as friends too rosy and starry eyed? I don't think so, if we remember we are talking about families where things are going fairly well. Of course not everyone can look back on a happy family life. Incest, abuse, abandonment, violence, and bitter divorces may mean that many individuals must leave their families behind and separate themselves from their relatives. In the previous chapter I talked of other serious conflicts and breakdowns that occur in families; it is a truism that not every family story has a happy ending.

I also recognize the fact that some parents may not want to be friends with their adult children; some people espouse a traditional form of filial piety in which more distant and respectful formal relationships are held to be proper. Popular American styles of informality and the culture's emphasis upon equality are not for them. Their traditions cannot bend or be abandoned. Well, so be it. You cannot create a friendship between people who resist the whole concept. I think these parents are missing something rich in life; but they might point out how much pain comes to parents who are so close to their children that they know all their troubles and are drawn into them. It's true that good communication with your children lets you hear things you sometimes might not want to hear, but that is the price paid for intimacy of any kind.

It is also well to remember that parent-child relationships that end up as friendly may have gone through rocky periods of friction and strain. Recuperating from the battles of a child's rebellious adolescence may take a decade or so. Reestablishing intimacy and getting to be friends as fellow adults can take effort after an estrangement. But in even the best cases talking with adult children is a disciplined art that has to be learned.

The Art of Conversing with Adult Children

If we want to end up as equal, mature adults who are friends as well as family, we have to treat our children in an adult manner. More to the point, parents have to stop the constant stream of instruction and educational correction necessary and appropriate for small children. To get down to a concrete case, suppose your twentysomething adult child eats like a pig when he — usually this will be a he — comes over to dinner. Should you as his parent complain or correct him?

I uphold as a guiding principle of communication with adult children what I call "the good friend test." This test is applied by asking yourself: "How might I approach a good friend in a similar situation?" The answers you come up with in this imaginative exercise help in handling conversations with adult children. If, for instance, I had an adult friend and beloved colleague who came to dinner frequently and did not conform to our family's American norms of table manners, how would I respond?

If my friend were an immigrant from another country with different customs I would certainly think it a favor to inform him tactfully about our American dining habits. I wouldn't want him to go blithely along in ignorance, offending people and risking social ostracism. At some point I'd privately give him the word about using knives and forks, or not grabbing food, or whatever he didn't know about our folkways.

But of course ignorance about proper behavior is not going to be the issue when it comes to your adult children. You, yourself, in the past have already told them, and told them, and reminded them yet once again about virtually everything they need to know. At an earlier stage of family life, parents are responsible for teaching Civilization and Etiquette 101. This course, which meets on a daily basis, always includes a unit on behavior at the dinner table, along with instructions on cleanliness, rules of dress, language use, punctuality, moral standards, and assorted other matters too numerous to mention. Repeated reviews and drills continue for a decade or more.

So in the good friend test, you have to imagine that your good friend knows how to behave, but still fails to conform to your family's customs. Then it becomes a matter of trying to decide what motivates this behavior (carelessness, defiance?) and deciding how much this behavior bothers you. During this period of reflection you would also consider whether the behavior is generalized to other settings and whether or not it would handicap your friend in other social situations. If the behavior really does bother you, and may have negative consequences for him as well, you might tactfully bring up the matter in private at some propitious moment. You would not, however, *not* automatically and preemptorily correct a fellow adult's manners at the table — not if you wanted to remain friends.

Obviously, I don't approve of parents who spontaneously nag, criticize, correct, and give directives to their adult children as if they were still in grade school. Adult families should be collegial, they are not the Marine Corps where ranking officers give commands and expect to be obeyed. Parents of adults do better to realize that it is too late to drum in elementary lessons in good behavior. If parents are seen as analogous to athletic coaches, as they have been, it makes no sense to still be running training drills when the game is in the third quarter. Parents who constantly criticize their adult children about their table manners, diet, hairstyles, grammar, clothes, and other shortcomings are assuming a parental prerogative that is only appropriate in an earlier stage of child rearing.

An adult is by definition in charge of his or her own behavior and all those things that are included in the dubious term "lifestyle." The only critique that seem appropriate for adult children, are the same tactful, delicate adult-to-adult communications you would use with a good friend. Yes, people who are true friends will speak up about sensitive personal topics and even tell their friends things that are painful to hear, for their own good. But such remarks are usually few and far between and reflected upon first. An effort should be made to be "as shrewd as a serpent, as innocent as a dove," as the Bible has it, and to employ a dove's gentle mode in the telling.

In fact, family relationships always do well to *exceed* the delicacy and thoughtfulness shown to friends — especially when adult children are involved. After all, the way a parent is treating a child is a socializing message in itself. Only small irresponsible children need to be controlled by their parents. Any adult who accepts parental criticisms given to them as if to a child, is reduced to a childish state — the very opposite of the maturity that the parent presumably hopes to encourage.

Adult children will rightly avoid parents who are still trying to exert control and ensure childlike passivity and obedience. As one of my sons describes it, "Unfortunately, lots of parents these days are into micromanagement of their grown children's lives." Micromanagement? Micromanagement, I found out, means minutely overseeing details and ensuring that all decisions conform to the master plan. Parents of adults infringe upon their children's adult status when they begin to direct and oversee the details of their children's daily lives. "Phone me before you go and after you get there," or "Did you fill out the graduate school application yet that I sent you?" And so on. When parents get controlling there will be trouble — either unhealthy regression to a dependent childlike state, defiant rebellion, or avoidance through distancing.

Yet at the same time some discussion of the details of another's life seems necessary for most friendships. Surely sharing the less than dramatic events of the day forms the basis of friendship and family life. Going over the minutia of life is part of intimacy. Parents, children, spouses, siblings, and friends are the only people who care enough to listen to one's experiences and be willing to see things from your own biased perspective.

I think the operative word here for parents is *listen.* Conversations driven only by a series of parental questions is not optimal communication. Truly flowing mutual talk can get short-circuited by criticisms, commands, premature problem solving, and psychological analyses of why one is having the reaction one displays.

There are many different conversational styles in the world, as has been noted by those who analyze how people talk to one another. There are ethnic differences, sex differences, regional differences, and power differentials in how people converse. Who initiates the talk, who can interrupt, what gets talked about? Is each person in the conversation equally free to say what he or she thinks? If parents want to have friendly conversations with their children they take to heart the idea that conversations have to be two-way, and full of mutual listening.

Friends, especially in woman-to-woman conversations, will encourage and enable the other person to talk and tell what he or she thinks and how he or she is feeling. Intimacy is built on the freedom to disclose personal information, personal opinions, or personal vulnerabilities — i.e., not having to play a role or keep up a front. It is a pretty thin relationship if we cannot comfort each other and share a laugh at the craziness of the world.

Parents who are friends with their adult children have learned to talk to them as they do to their friends. Fathers may find this more difficult to do since few men have any friends to speak of, and even when a man has a friend, male talk is often not very personal but oriented instead to problem solving and comments on sports, business, and politics. Many men also claim that they become friends by doing things together. This may work for many fathers and children as well, but when parents don't live close to their children, or regularly work or socialize together, the male approach to friendship will not be adequate. A father is handicapped if his conversation with a child is limited to a check on their finances, job status, general health, and transportation arrangements. Instrumental problem-solving discourse breaks down if there isn't a problem to solve.

To get going in a friendship with children, a father, or sometimes a micromanaging mother, may have to learn new ways of speaking — almost a new dialect. Parents willing to change can practice a few tried-and-true techniques. Read something together and talk about it. Ask advice about a problem, reveal self-doubts, express a personal regret, or a fond hope, and listen, listen, listen. Paralanguage, gestures, and body language are important in facilitating dialogue or inhibiting it. We should all be forced to see ourselves on videotape; then we would notice the messages we are conveying with our "unhuns," "mmms," tightened lips, glazed eyes, or on the other hand, friendly pats, nodding heads, and beaming smiles. Within families, we are all so attuned to the smallest signals that emotional vibrations in the air and the way we say things are as important as what we say. Brrr, watch out when the pots in the kitchen are being banged around in a certain way. The medium is the message, and should be attended to.

Women are often adept in the enabling mode of conversation because they are more practiced in intimate friendships. Unlike men, women know enough to ask directions when they are lost, so of course they have a head start in becoming friends with adult children. Since this is usually so, it is important for women not to monopolize family communication. In too many American homes when the phone rings and it is the husband's mother or sister, or his adult son or daughter, the man answers, says hail and farewell, and hands his wife the phone. She is in charge of chatting and conversation, and is then supposed to relay the family news to her husband; she is the eternal go-between. Breaking out of these patterns, when they exist, is possible.

It is beneficial for everyone in a family, if the individuals can spend time together one-on-one. Fathers and sons, even the silent types, can learn to talk and enjoy it. So many parents complain that after marriage takes place, they never get to talk to their adult children alone anymore, particularly their sons. Why can't everyone in the family have individual time alone to sing some duets? It's much more satisfying than a constant program of singing with the general chorus.

Affectionate playfulness in conversation is important for family fun. Fond in-group jokes and running comedy routines are found in happy families. Hostile teasing and competitive jabs, on the other hand, can be unpleasant and debilitating. Doing things together, as in male friendships, is also a wonderful way to encourage closeness, when accompanied by relaxed conversation. Rich families take the whole family on a cruise as crew, or invite the family to go hiking in the Himalayas; the rest of us can take walks together and help each other paint and garden. Many parents in dispersed families do not have much chance to spend a great deal of time with adult children. The question of frequency of contact and communication becomes another troubling issue.

How Frequently Do Parents and Children Talk?

Once at a New York dinner party I heard a mother surprise the assembled guests when she announced that she talked to her two adult daughters every day, and sometimes more. Every Day??? This much contact is rare in many of today's mobile families. But daily contact is often taken for granted in traditional families who live near each other. An older father I know said that each of his three adult daughters called home every day. "We just think it is their place to do so," he said. This close Italian family of parents and daughters also worked together occasionally in a family business and there was a great deal of mutual visiting and cooperation.

Other parents report that the amount of contact with their adult children differs depending on the child. Daughters tend to stay in closer contact than sons, but not always. Some parents may talk weekly to one or more of their children and not talk much at all with other more elusive offspring. Some children are more extroverted or family oriented or just stick around more than others. Even when relationships are basically good, some adult children are not too communicative. They may show up for family holidays and events but not stay in constant contact.

Often adult children get immersed in their work or their own frantic round of activities. Those that are unmarried may be less oriented to family values and call less frequently. When marriage comes and a grandchild appears it often seems to up the communication quotient. Who else is as interested in the marvels of a new baby as his or her fond relatives? My own explanation of the grandchild effect is that the first days of parenthood bring a thunderclap of revelation: "My God, someone went through this for me!" One's eyes are opened, and thereafter all parents, including one's own, are looked at with new respect. Until you've tried it, you take parenting for granted.

Communication is also more difficult if children have moved far away, or the parents have moved away. Here much depends on the motivation for the move. We all know adult children who have moved as far away as possible in order to distance themselves physically and psychologically from parents they consider a toxic influence. If they could have a parentectomy they would. In other cases the parents and children have become separated before they were ever able to move into an adult friendship relationship. Frequent contact has faded and lapsed.

There are also parents who have been disappointed, or worse, by their adult children. As noted in previous discussions of conflict, parents can deliberately break off communication. Other parents flee the scene for different, more subtle reasons. I know of several cases in which parents have left their homes with adult children still ensconced. Separation or finding "severance points" in today's parent-child relationship is not always easy. Mother bears just disappear and leave yearling bear cubs to fend for themselves when it's time; young adult offspring know about forwarding addresses. One couple I know of volunteered for overseas employment and sold their stateside house in order to push their adult children into greater efforts toward self-reliance.

The right words to describe some adult children are hard to find: "stagnating?" "stalled?" "paralyzed?" One drastic therapy is to cut down on contact for a while.

In satisfactory parent-child relationships the communication rate is usually adjusted to fit the different personalities and family folkways. Talking every day may anchor one end of the continuum, particularly between mothers and daughters, or between fathers and sons who work together in a family business. Once a week or every ten days may be more or less what most other parents can count on. I am on a once every ten days call or visit schedule with most of my children, with extra time awarded for holidays and special family events. But I am the pursuer, the one who usually initiates the calls. Of course right now both my husband and I travel a lot and we are pretty engrossed in our work. If I lived alone or needed company more I would feel free to call my children more often, just as they step up their communication when there is some crisis in their lives or they think I need support.

I also know of families who love each other, but just aren't particularly chatty. Surely the taciturn Scandinavians of Lake Woebegone are not going to run up phone bills like talkative Southerners or Jewish mothers. There are still some people in this country who do not feel comfortable talking by long distance phone. The long distance phone call, like a telegram, signals bad news and a dire emergency. At the other extreme of technological ingenuity some dispersed families have mastered new video and taping techniques so that they routinely communicate by sending tapes. Many of these technologies have taken the place of letter writing — a long lost skill. On the whole emotionally close families seem to work out their own rhythms of communication in ways that suit them.

When a parent wants more communication and an adult child resists, then this is another example of a sensitive matter that can benefit from using the good friend test. How would I broach such a difference of opinion with a good friend? I certainly wouldn't demand that they call or visit more, or nag them about their failure to do so. I might tell them that it made me sad that we didn't have more contact, and urge them to come more often. But I would be afraid that by pushing too hard, I might transform our friendship into a duty to be reluctantly fulfilled. As a parent I would never play the card of filial piety and duty unless I faced a serious need for help. But by that time the equality and inter-dependence of the middle period of parenting would probably be over anyway, and we would be entering the endgame of old age, illness, and death.

In the middle years when parents and their children are equal adults, we can aim to be friends who freely meet because we enjoy each other. This will continue to be the case if we have learned how to weather times of conflict.

Difficult Communication and "The Discipline of the Tongue"

One mother that I know had her thirtysomething married son de-liver an accolade to her out of the blue. "Mom, I want to thank you for never interfering or telling Mary Anne and me what to do or how to raise Frankie." Happily surprised, this mother replied, "I knew that if you had wanted my advice you would have asked for it." This mother, as a matter of fact, had never really disap-proved of anything her fine son and admirable daughter-in-law did, so her restraint was not difficult. On further reflection how-ever, she allowed as how if she had been in charge she might have done a few things differently, but "I was smart enough to bite my tongue and keep quiet."

In medieval spirituality, individuals seeking perfection were enjoined to cultivate "the discipline of the tongue." This meant that through proper exercises of self-control, a person will not say what is better left unsaid, and only say those words that serve love and truth. "Justice and kindness shall kiss" as the Biblical Psalm puts it. Parents who are successful in the art of talking to their adult children have become adepts in the discipline of the tongue. Their initial efforts to learn to be quiet can be exhausting but it gets easier with practice. The other side of this discipline is of course learning how to speak up when it is appropriate and engage in conflict when it is necessary.

Even in the best of relationships some conflict is inevitable. Parents and adult children who are friends will still have to work out differences. An example of relatively mild parent-adult child conflict might be over whether a vacation or Easter visit from children will, or will not, be forthcoming, or whether parents should give up their house and move to an apartment. As for the latter dilemma, some adult children might urge their parents to simplify their life, others nostalgically resist the symbolic passing of their childhood.

But parents will either move or not, children will either visit or not. Once the debated issue is resolved in one way or another, it is over. One or the other in the parent-child dyad either disregarded the other's advice or was persuaded to adopt the other person's point of view. If one's decision turns out to be wrong it is an act of real friendship and an exercise of the discipline of the tongue to refrain from second guessing and recriminations. Family members make mistakes like all the world, but home should be a place where forgiveness and tolerance of human error is found.

Things are more difficult if there is parent-child conflict over a serious important issue that cannot be resolved. One type of serious, ongoing conflict is ideological: the bone of contention is moral, religious, or political beliefs. I will talk in the last chapter about these serious conflicts over central values and beliefs. I grew up in a Southern military family of lapsed Calvinists and by the time I was an adult my father and I had ended up disagreeing over a whole range of ideological issues — over race, religion, politics, careers, and money. We disagreed over every life decision I made, from becoming a Christian, to the college I chose, to the husband I married, to my decisions to have so many children. Yet we loved each other deeply and learned in the end to get along.

Not surprisingly I have adult children who rebel against many of my beliefs. My experience of life in an America full of intra-family pluralism is that it is possible to love and befriend persons with whom you seriously disagree. Of course you have to respect those with whom you differ, and want to get along. One effective strategy for keeping the family peace is "the method of avoidance," another aspect of the discipline of the tongue. In order to prevent constant conflict and fighting over an incendiary issue both parties voluntarily avoid raising the issue or pursuing the subject when it comes up.

At some point there will have been a protracted argument that establishes the fact that you and your child are in serious disagreement. Let us say the argument is over the Gulf War or abortion or religious truth or homosexual marriage, or whatever. After the first protracted conflict it becomes clear that neither person is changing his or her position; so then both debaters back off and avoid further combat. Whenever the topic is raised there is a pause, followed by a joking dismissal and change of subject.

Unfortunately when there are numerous differences resulting in too much avoidance of too many subjects, parent-child conversations can become excessively boring. (This is also true of marital relations as well.) Too much of what really matters to both parties has to be avoided and be kept off limits. Families that never mention anything that might provoke conflict run the danger that deeply personal communications will grind to a halt. Trivialities and routine superficialities have to take the place of all meaningful subjects. Or as Edith Wharton wrote describing a stultifying Old New York family encounter, "But, as it was against all the rules of their code that the mother and son should ever allude to what was uppermost in their thoughts, he simply replied: 'Oh, well, there's always a phase of family parties to be gone through when one gets engaged, and the sooner it's over the better.' "

To avoid such excesses of denial, "where the real thing was never said or done or even thought" (Wharton again), family members must be ready to engage in occasional quick clean fights and spirited skirmishes. People keep awake, engaged, and on their toes if they know that every now and then a passionately felt shot is coming across the bow. The conversation erupts into a rapid exchange of fire, and then the two vessels, like the *Monitor* and the *Merrimack*, disengage and sail away into the tranquil sea. A little excitement, or even incitement, keeps a parent-child relationship authentic amid the general agreement to maintain the peace.

Many a member of a contentious clan has reported that after a sharp exchange or two there was an increase of telephone calls and affectionate avowals — not exactly apologies rendered, but an effort to mend fences and keep the bonds of respect and affection in good condition.

Apologies, retractions, and admissions are, of course, other crucial ingredients for any friendly relationship. When you change your mind you should say so: "All right, I've thought it over and you've convinced me," or "I'm sorry I got so irritable," or "I was carried away and want to take back what I said about ———." If parents cannot make admissions of error or apologies to their adult children, they cannot be friends. Parents as founders and mentors of the family should be models of civility. It may be hard for adult children to become secure enough to admit that *they* were wrong, but without the example of their parents, it will be harder.

My father, my friend and antagonist, always claimed that he was right and that furthermore, he had never been wrong in his entire life — but then came his roar of laughter, giving the lie to his outrageous boast. More often he would regale us with accounts of the mistakes he had made as a naive but arrogant young sailor far from his Alabama home. Self-deprecating country humor ended every tale. The underlying message to us was (1) even you, wonderful, smart, and intelligent as you are, do not know everything, and (2) learn from experience. I try to convey this same message to my children.

In the family we are on a trek together and I plan to keep learning. I am willing, if not always delighted, to be corrected and get all the help I can from my family and friends. What do you know that I should know? Talk. I promise to listen carefully; in any conflict I will make it my business to be sure that I can state your position as well as I can state my own. You tell me your thoughts and I'll tell you mine.

In the family one can work toward that utopian goal, "the ideal speech-situation": that is, an ongoing lifetime of conversation with no ulterior motives, no deception, no unfair exercises of power to keep anyone from having their say. Playing fair is important. Each person should be able to be equally assertive and speak up. In American society we sometimes have the ironic situation that it is the parents who find it harder to state their needs than their adult children do. Parents may have always been the nurturers and not yet learned to receive or ask anything from their children. But surely asking for things you want is also necessary in a friendship.

Messages from various movements of assertiveness training have now penetrated the land. Many people today have absorbed much of the popular but basically useful self-help advice about how to communicate better — as one-minute managers and so on. And these strategies work in family exchanges too. We now know we should say "I think, I want, ———," rather than "You always ———." Starting with what you know to be true about yourself keeps you from infuriating the other person by arrogantly assuming that your interpretation of what he or she is doing and why must be infallibly accepted. If all members of the family learn to assert themselves instead of being aggressive and hostile, dialogue improves.

There is one important point that parents need to be assertive about after they have learned to listen to and befriend their adult children. Parents should not accept their children's efforts to blame them for problems that their adult children encounter in the present. Epidemics of parent-blaming are abroad in the land and are an unhealthy sign of regressions to adolescence on the part of young adults. If parental mistakes were made in the past — and what parent doesn't make mistakes? — now that a child is an adult it's his or her turn to take hold and responsibly get on with his or her future. Adult children are responsible for shaping their own moral character; parents did not in the past ever exercise complete control and they certainly do not now control the choices that their adult children make.

Mature persons are interested in becoming good parents, good citizens, good workers, not in brooding over their childhoods in an effort to assign guilt to others who may have injured them. If adults do not like the way their parents did things, let them live differently and work for a better future. Let them have children of their own. I've always resented people who write and complain about their inadequate mothers, or fathers, who have never ventured to have children. A woman can hardly understand, "my mother, my self," until she lives the other side in the relationship and has a child of her own. Parents should not let their adult children get away with infantile fantasies that since they were entitled to perfect parents and ideal childhoods their parents should accept perpetual guilt. This sense of narcissism is as damaging to family life as those parents who demand perfection in their adult children. It isn't good for any mature adult to cultivate victim status and pursue pseudomartyrdom.

In some families the sacrificial bending of one's own will and desires to others has become a bad habit on the part of both generations. Something as simple as deciding where to go for dinner can become a tortuous problem if everyone is excessively, evasively polite and won't assert a preference. In these and similar cases it becomes impossible to negotiate any decision because no one can tell what the others actually want. You may end up where no one wants to be, with pouting and sulking thrown in for good measure. Silence can be a form of manipulation if the hidden agenda is that everyone else has to guess what I want and give it to me without my asking. If you love me, read my mind.

Silence about hidden family secrets can also be corrosive. Repressing shameful secrets is different from a conscious decision to be quiet in order to avoid fruitless conflict tactfully. As we have come to see in the last decades the ability to disclose secret wounds and talk about them is a first step in healing. Incest survivors for instance, with the worst family secret imaginable, begin to heal when they can talk to sympathetic others about what happened to them. When some horrible confusing trauma can be put into words, it loses demonic power to overwhelm the mind. If the unspeakable experience is no longer denied and can be formulated in speech, it is no longer seen as uncontrollable. Telling painful secrets is good for your mental and physical health.

As with big secrets so with smaller ones. Mentioning the family's problematic and hidden problems can remove pressure on everyone. An alcoholic grandfather or a retarded sibling, once acknowledged, moves everyone in the family closer to reality. There may, of course, be some limits to disclosure as one maintains a delicate balance between sharing one's own secrets and breaking the confidences of others. No rule will apply to every situation. But erring on the side of openness within the family seems the better course. While overt fights and recognized conflicts can be engaged in and then consciously avoided for the sake of peace, unmentionable facts around which everyone must tiptoe create permanent roadblocks to communication. It is a relief no longer to have to bear in mind what must not be mentioned.

Who can understand others unless they know the shadows and suffering that go into a life as well as the joys and triumphs? There are civilized rules against littering the environment with self-pity, but too much stoicism is off-putting as well. It may be magnificently self-controlled never, ever to complain or bring up painful events. But such shows of strength are not the best way to build friendships with one's children. Friendship and communication is built upon sharing the lights and the shadows of personal experience.

CHAPTER FOUR

Careers, Jobs, and Honest Work:
It Isn't Just the Money

They should put "an ability to do career counseling" in the parental job description packet! One mother reported that her son's nine-month job search after coming home from graduate school was worse than any pregnancy she had undergone. She and her husband made efforts to support their son before job interviews and after disappointing rejections but it was not clear that anything was of any help. In a depressed economic scene it is no easy feat for a young person to get a good job, or for parents to maintain cheerful confidence and benign detachment from the process.

As the weeks of unemployment mounted these parents had to stave off mounting doubts. Had they raised a son who could not compete in the marketplace? James was making money as a skilled painter of houses but his efforts to find work in his professional field were meeting with no success. Was it really a problem of bad times or did their son have some problem with competition and self-presentation? It does not always help to know that jobs in general are scarce, because if anyone is getting work out there, parents can reason that their son should be able to do so as well.

Anxieties over jobs are a new and strange problem for a generation of parents who started their own careers in boom times. In an earlier day all you needed to get a good job was proof of your educational preparation and a demonstration of good will. If you did your part and went to a decent school, many opportunities awaited you. In these more competitive times of recession and depression getting started in a career and keeping a job can be a struggle. The outlook is particularly tough for what is known as "the trailing edge" of baby boomers, those born from 1955 to 1964.

James's parents were hard pressed to try to think up helpful strategies and advice, and to remain encouraging. They did not have any contacts or connections in their son's chosen field so they could not help him get an interview. This mother felt particularly worried in this crisis because the siblings of this hardworking eldest son, who had toiled through the established path of graduate school, were watching his job search with some skepticism. If James couldn't get a job after doing everything right, why should they buckle down to more years of education?

James finally got a good job in his field after months of trying, but the stress accompanying this all too typical job search provides several lessons. The obvious one might be that everyone today needs a backup subsistence skill, like painting or typing, to support periods of unemployment in his or her profession. Another moral that is penetrating the middle class for the first time is how important it can be for young people to be able to look forward to work opportunities. Suddenly the high unemployment statistics of the ghetto, the barrio, or northern Ireland, become more of a reality. It can happen here.

Joblessness is a social plague that induces a crippling sense of helplessness and dependency. It is frightening to read that, at age twenty-nine, nearly 40 percent of American men have failed to find a stable, long-term job. Young men and women are taking longer to get established, and tend to return home when unemployed or in the throes of career changes or after being laid off, or "excessed." Parents who are secure enough not to have to worry about their own employment find themselves footing the bills for the returnees' room and board, as well as contributing to tuition for adult children entering graduate school as they change careers.

Parents may have tried very hard to keep their children from graduating college without a crushing load of student debt. Some affluent parents succeed, but for others it may be impossible. But when an expensive graduate school tuition is added on, young adult debt becomes a hidden social reality. It is a shadow deficit weighing down the initial stages of a young person's working life. The pressure to pay back expensive student loans gets added on to other strains surrounding work and careers. Getting a job becomes urgent.

Few parents can guarantee a job or successfully stage-manage a career for a son or daughter. Gone are the days when parents could help provide for their children's livelihood by arranging apprenticeships or entry jobs at the parental place of work or at a friend of the family's business. Nepotism is frowned upon except in the building and plumbing trades or in the remaining family businesses. And who has a farm to pass on to children anymore? Parents can help pay for schooling and if they are very fortunate they can provide contacts and family connections to gain an entry interview, or more rarely an entry level job, but little else.

Adult children have to make it on their own. One private tale that became public knowledge involved the continuing efforts made by a distinguished New York judge to help her difficult daughter, Sukhreet, get and keep a job. After a series of unsuccessful attempts at different lines of work Sukhreet obtained a job as an assistant to Bess Meyerson in her city government post. Unfortunately, a full-scale scandal erupted when the judge was accused of bending her legal rulings in the divorce case of Meyerson's lover in exchange for her daughter's employment. While the judge was finally exonerated, many parents of adult children could sympathize with this sad story of a successful and respected mother desperately trying to help her floundering daughter find employment. Two achieving career parents do not necessarily produce achieving children.

Unlike youngsters, or even adolescents, young adults have to make their own way in the adult world of jobs and careers. Adult offspring must find honest, meaningful work and at the same time support themselves. In the process all sorts of family beliefs and heretofore hidden assumptions and convictions about work and careers may produce unexpected intergenerational conflicts.

Parents who were prepared for counseling about college decisions and prepared to give encouragement and support in persevering to graduation, are not ready for their extended roles as career counselors. Parents watching from the sidelines as their children enter the world of employment are forced to rethink their own ideas and review their experiences and expectations about work and careers.

In the workplace an adult has to succeed with an employer and with peers and colleagues who are not willing to treat him or her with the loving forbearance of a family member. Success at work takes sustained effort as well as individual talent and intelligence. Ambition and conscientious effort have to be complemented by the individual's ability to get along and cooperate with others.

Personality deficiencies and social inadequacies probably play a greater part in failed careers than lack of competence. When middle-aged persons think of the promising young persons they started out with, those who fell by the wayside often were unsuccessful at work because of personality problems. (I include drinking too much as a personality problem!) Work requires self-discipline, self-control, perseverance, and endurance — all internal traits of individual character. Freud said a healthy person has the ability to love and to work, but these are abilities that no one can supply for others, no matter how much you love them or how hard you have worked to give them their chance in life.

Parents will have had their own encounters with work and have their attitudes affected by their own work histories. They may have been successful, happy, and challenged in their work, or just plodded along in order to make a living. Unfortunately, some American workers have been frustrated, thwarted, and broken by drudgery in unfair labor conditions. Whatever the parent's own experience of work, most parents will have hopes for their children's work lives. The American dream has always been to see your children find good work that is more respected and more remunerative than your own.

Most Americans have been prepared to pay the price involved in having one's child get more education than they did and move up in the class system. A father who has been a factory worker cannot have firsthand experiences of what his son, the college professor, meets in his working conditions. If there has been an education gap the father and mother may find it impossible to advise a child who faces entirely new decisions in a more technical field. But an immigrant and internally migrating people is prepared for this kind of distancing between the generations, however painful it may be. The parents are proud that their children have problems they can't understand. It is part of the American dream to see one's children fly up, up, and away.

Yet dreams are smashed quite regularly. Individual children may not succeed in work because of their own incapacities, but hard times can ensure that even the most talented and hard-working young adults won't get a fair chance to succeed in a career. Parents can have fears and anxieties over the future as they see more and more good workers fired or laid off during a recession or depression. The thought that your offspring will do worse than you did in the world of work is painful. Downward mobility for offspring means that the quantity and quality of work available to them, and the money they can earn doing it, will be less than that of their parents.

Until I got a good look at the current young-adult squeeze I don't think I had been cognizant of how fortunate my husband and I have been in having meaningful work. I have never done anything I didn't think was intrinsically worthwhile, from twenty years of child rearing and homemaking to psychotherapy, teaching, and writing. My husband has been equally lucky. As unalienated workers, we have worked hard and upheld the work ethic as a central value of life. It is important to us that our children be good workers and find honest, meaningful work.

Some of the most traumatic fights we have ever had with several of our children have been over work. To be able-bodied but lazy, unfocused, and unwilling to work seems more or less unforgivable in our household. It isn't simply a matter of making money, although work and money are related, but adhering to a standard of hard work is a mark of maturity; a good worker is willing to do his or her share in the family and in the society. In these family struggles over work, I used to put up on the icebox, the central bulletin board of the modern home, St. Paul's maxim, "He who does not work, neither let him eat." If an adult able-bodied child refused to work or look for work, then there was bound to be a parting of the ways.

Why do parents like myself get so exercised about the need to work and to find good work? Obviously, work is important because it is the only way for an adult to earn money and be self-sufficient; and it is the only way for a person to be able to provide for others, or to offer others hospitality. But more than this, a person who works is an agent acting in the world, instead of remaining a passive drifter. Self-esteem comes from work well done; self-absorbed loungers and dilettantes never have this experience of hard-earned competence after struggle.

At work you learn to cooperate with others and take part in the grown-up world where difficulties have to be overcome with persevering effort. A narcissistic sense of entitlement and omnipotence left over from childhood gets transformed. The great psychologist Piaget said that adolescence lasts until you go to work. The immature person who cannot stand to be bored or to delay personal gratification cannot work well.

Parents who value work for all these reasons can face a range of unexpected challenges. Surprisingly enough, lazy, drifting, confused, or incompetent workers are not the only parental concern. To start with a more subtle problem and at the opposite extreme of career counseling challenges, there are families in which adult children overdo the work ethic.

Workaholic Overachievers

"My daughter works a seventy-hour week, she makes great money but she has no life"; this testimony from a mother of a young businesswoman is typical. Such adult children do not have to be convinced of the value of work. They not only have taken the American work ethic to heart but have embraced it to an extreme degree. These young adults work all the time; their lives seem completely consumed by their careers. Of course, these go-getters and high achievers make their parents proud by their successes. Usually they are also making piles of money, so they will obtain financial self-sufficiency without a problem, paying back their student loans promptly. But parents worry if work is taking over all the rest of a child's life. Family, friends, politics, religion, culture, and leisure can be scanted when a young person spends most of his or her time and energy at work.

In the familiar jargon of the day we call patterns of compulsive overwork "workaholism." This unhealthy condition exists when people let their work deform their personalities and crowd out all other relationships and activities of life. Workaholics seem to become addicted to work much younger than they used to, often before young persons have been able to find a mate or have a family or make ties within a community or neighborhood. Capable young people on the fast track, in highly competitive fields, are often pressured and seduced into overwork and careerism. Young attorneys work high-pressured eighty-hour work weeks in a highly remunerated form of chattel slavery. They belong to the firm, body and soul.

All Americans work on an average of 163 more hours per year now then in 1970. People in middle-class America work harder and longer than they would have dreamed of doing back in the fifties. More is demanded. Partly this is economic. The high rewards, and high anxiety about falling behind, or being fired, reinforce work obsessions. Everywhere we see the symptoms of stress that accompany a harried life in the fast lane. But partly our obsession with work is an impoverishment of culture problem. Once I was telling one of my colleagues that primitive people only worked three to four hours to maintain themselves. A worried look of incredulity came over his face, "But what did they do with themselves the rest of the time?" he asked. "Oh you know," I said "they visited back and forth, carved and painted, played games, worshiped, had holiday customs, made music and had fun." This thoroughly modern man had never read that leisure is the basis of all culture, so I gave up.

Success, partly symbolized by money earned, is still the jealous bitch goddess of America. Parents of young workaholics can wonder if they helped induct their children into this consuming cult of success and achievement. Parents in mid-life may reflect upon their own past and wonder whether they too were driven in their earlier work patterns. Certainly many older men of high achievement regret that they did not pay as much attention to their children as they should have when the children were growing up. Career women also worry whether their determination to be Wonderwoman may have been costly to their children. Such regrets over earlier career choices can engender worries over a grown child's work obsession.

If, however, parents were always thwarted in their work, they may sense that they have subtly pressed their children to make up for their own deficiencies. Those who failed at work and careers may invest heavily in their offspring's success. Women who never had the opportunities for careers may push their daughter's career achievements. The temptation is always there for parents to push adult children into fulfilling their own hidden or not so hidden agendas.

When daughters and sons are too consumed by work to find a mate, or too involved in their work to have children, parents may worry. But isn't this worry just another hidden parental agenda coming to the fore? Yes, the selfish thought does arise that the biological clock is ticking away one's chances for in-laws and grandchildren, but more altruistic concerns can also be on a parent's mind. Will my child who is so caught up today in a career, miss out in the long run on having a family of his or her own? Parents who are renewed by their relationships with their grown children are saddened by the possibility that their children may miss this rich experience for themselves. Social analysts have noted that many people now turn their work situations into substitute families with daddy and mommy bosses and sibling coworkers. These observations do not give parents in a young adult's real family much comfort.

The prevalence of our obsession with work and achievement in America creates what has been called a harried leisure class. No other elite in history has ever worked such long hours. Have we really progressed all that much from a society in which perpetual drudgery was a curse and unceasing toil took its toll in health and happiness? Today fancier forms of competition and overwork are doing damage to our leisure, family life, and communities. The mediating institutions of life, from family to churches, to neighborhood associations, to service clubs and political parties, are based upon volunteers expending energy and time that is not job related. The public sphere and the common good suffer when the best and the brightest are too busy to help build the good society.

Parents who have had time to reflect on the balance between work, leisure, and family life can help their adult children truly value work and the work ethic and yet keep it in its place. Like little bear's porridge, the commitment to work should not be either too hot or too cold, but just right. Getting the right mix of work and the rest of life can be an ongoing project. Family discussions, family exemplars and family support can help adult children fight against the mindless pressures of the times.

Faltering Workers

"Workaholism" is far from the problems that other parents face. There are other adult children who refuse to buckle down or to commit themselves seriously to either a career or a trade. They remain unfocused and faltering workers. These laggards from the work ethic appear in many different varieties. There are out-and-out manipulative lazy types who are fairly easy to spot. Clearly they should not be enabled to pursue feckless patterns of sponging for money or subsidies. They will live out the family pattern of "from shirtsleeves to shirtsleeves in three generations."

A more ambiguous situation, however, arises when adult children are romantic idealists, who rebel against meaningless work and the materialistic competition of the fast track. They do not wish to get up to speed. Young adults may more or less drop out, retreat to Vermont or California and engage in subsistence living, perhaps with an easygoing pursuit of arts, crafts, music, in fellowship with like-minded souls.

Often a young person's rebellion against work and the work ethic reflects the yearnings and ideals of parents who in their youth had no choice but to struggle to make a living. We should remember that in colonial times the hard-working John Adams proclaimed that he was a farmer and politician so his children could be educated professionals, so that their children in turn could be poets and artists. Some might say that the Adams family steadily declined as the generations moved from John and Abigail to Henry and Clover.

The goal of cultivated leisure, however, remains an aristocratic ideal handed down to us from the Greeks by way of the British upper classes. Their rejection of those "in trade," who actually worked for a living, was reflected in the maxim that it took three generations to make a gentleman. The first generation makes the money, the second learns upper-class ways, and by the third generation a young man has so thoroughly forgotten the hard-working scramble for the family fortune that he takes a gentleman's leisured culture for granted. Manual labor was thought to be particularly polluting.

This ideal of privileged leisure was generally incompatible with the American work ethic, but has always retained its champions and practitioners. The cultivated person as Renaissance man and amateur has been one minor American cultural type. Edith Wharton's novels of Old New York society are full of these representatives of solid families who enjoyed the dilettante's life. Henry James, Wharton's great friend, boasted that no one in his family had worked for a living in the last three generations.

Many of today's well-educated parents were taught to admire a leisured life devoted to creative art and literature. Yet in reality a life devoted to creating art demands years of highly focused, disciplined effort. The life of an artist is hard, and quite different from the undisciplined life of the dabbling dilettante. Without supreme dedication, along with good fortune, an artist can never have a successful career, much less hope to come near financial independence. Many great artists lived in near poverty and only survived because of generous patronage.

And who will be the modern equivalent of a patron? A young adult's parent? Parents who have adult children pursuing the arts are faced with interesting judgment calls. Is my child really talented and is his or her pursuit of an artistic career a truly disciplined dedicated effort or is it a way of evading work and responsibility? It is hard to tell. In the meantime young adults leading Bohemian, alternate life-styles do not have job security, long-term benefits, or even immediate protection against hospitalization or illness. As one parent said ruefully, "I never thought I would become so fixated on health insurance and job benefits."

Parents can find themselves paying for their struggling adult children's health insurance. Should they? Is this really their problem? Alas, yes — it can be. Affluent parents know that if their son or daughter faced a medical emergency they would not be able to stand by and see their child denied adequate treatment; they would end up footing the bill. So in a way, it is a parental problem, and parents end up paying for health insurance in self-defense. But it can be depressing to confront an adult child's inability to earn money, and/or their lack of foresight or insight into economic realities.

The old parable of the ant and the grasshopper becomes relevant. Middle-class young adults who choose an alternative life-style with shaky economic security often can aspire to such paths because of their parents' conformity and success in the system. The prudent toiling ant has made the life of the grasshopper possible; but mindful of what happens to grasshoppers in the winter, should the ant continue to pay? How long should well-to-do, hard-working parents subsidize their young adult child's aspirations for creative work?

Much depends upon how hard the young adult works at his or her craft, and how probable are the chances for success. Outside assessment by persons in the field may be one way to know whether a young adult has talent or a real chance. In some fields like acting and music, the odds are stacked against anyone's being able to make it. Waiting for the big break may become futile. The more prudent life course is to find a backup way to make a living, in alternate scenarios such as teaching.

Many parents have found it necessary to cut the purse strings and end their role as patrons of unsuccessful artistic careers or other idealistic ventures. They make the justifiable demand that their adult child find work that may not be as artistically fulfilling, but can provide an adequate living in the long run. Honest work serves the good purpose of provisioning one's self and others, even if it is boring. The dignity of work, which is not illegal or destructive, comes from the human person who works to meet human needs.

At some point parental economic support given in the cause of finding the perfect career can become a handicapping prop for prolonging behavior that is immature and maladaptive. It is an old and painful pattern to see self-made parents who labored and struggled for their success, weaken their children by overprotecting and overindulging them. The fair-haired and thoroughly cosseted young prince or princess can become a failed adult who cannot move from entitlement to giving to others. If there are dependents or children involved, the duty to work is increased. To choose to make an artistic statement and sacrifice material goods for one's self is one thing, to deprive one's family of necessities is reprehensible.

How Can Parents Help Their Children as Workers?

Parents can support healthy attitudes toward work, recognizing that having good work is a primary goal of life, but not the only goal. But how is this done? One interesting feature of parenting adults is that any influence you wield is almost all psychological and not bound by time pressures or rigid rules. With the variety of individual cases presented in the plethora of parent-child relationships there can be few general rules about what to convey about work or how to talk about it. A parent as an observer can pay close attention to an adult child as a unique individual and mull over the opportunities and concrete challenges a child faces.

Parents with a high regard for the work ethic may look with a jaundiced eye upon many of the existing jobs and careers in the society. One of the requirements for good work is that it be honest and that it be a challenge to the worker's talents and that it serve the good of the society as well as the individual. Can we admire jobs and careers that minister to greed or serve socially destructive purposes, no matter how much they pay? Finding remunerative work that is worth doing and that matches a particular individual's gifts and talents is not an easy task. Law and medicine, those tried and true routes to doing well while doing good, are no longer surefire solutions to the problem of finding good work. Many idealistic Harvard law graduates stream out of law firms to find a better way of life. They are not satisfied if their working lives are going to be spent making rich people richer or defending the interests of big corporations in the society. Young physicians are not able to be the healers that they may have dreamed of being. Many of the best and the brightest young adults end up in surreal work settings like that depicted by Tom Wolfe in the novel *The Bonfire of the Vanities*. The hero never actually makes anything but is constantly on the phone and at his computer terminal making complex financial deals. He works in a crowded room noisy with the sound of "young men baying for money." He cannot possibly explain to his daughter (or to his wife) what he actually does at work.

So often there is a conflict between what the society esteems and monetarily rewards and what is a socially useful productive occupation. Many parents would rather see their child work as a teacher in a slum school or as a skilled carpenter or nurse than be highly paid in another line of work. It is not their decision to make, of course, but they may believe that while it is true that poverty and joblessness can make you miserable, money and a high status job cannot make you happy. Ideally, a person should like each day of work for its own sake, and think that the ultimate purposes of the work is also worthwhile. Work is too important and takes too many hours of one's allotted days on earth to pursue useless deadening tasks if others are available.

But there are many socially useful jobs and careers; which one should a person choose? There is a tyranny of choice in modern lives. Unless an individual has an outstanding talent, choosing a career can be confusing. Parents can help their children find their way, at least by urging them not to go along mindlessly with the crowd to business school or law school unless it seems right for them. If something is not right, the family can again play its buffering role between work and the individual. If a family is willing to offer support then a person can quit a program or leave a job to try to find more satisfying work — at least once. If the child is hard-working and disciplined, parents are willing to help them choose the most suitable line of work.

Today we cannot ship offspring off to the frontier or to the colonies to make their way. Detachment and just the right amount of support and aid have to be forthcoming in more complicated circumstances and at closer quarters. But once the young adult has found a career opportunity, what specific support can parents give as their adult child adjusts to a new work situation?

One of the best forms of support for another adult is listening. A new worker is trying to make his or her way in a new and confusing system with its own positive and negative elements. A parent can offer a sounding board and sympathetic ear to tales of the office or workplace. It is often disillusioning to enter the world of work and find out that grown-ups so often act like children and that in some settings little work is conscientiously or capably done. In competitive jobs and offices there may be antagonisms and office politics that can be a shock to an entering novice.

Parents can offer support and tentative advice culled from their own experiences of coming to terms with the imperfect world of employment. There is always a necessary balance between counseling rebellious nonconformity and counseling accommodation. If each worker's family is a buffer and a reinforcing bulwark against unjust exploitation at work, then whistleblowing or assertiveness about any kind of harassment (sexual or otherwise) is possible.

One mother told her daughter in California that she would send support money after she heard that her daughter's boss had ordered her daughter, as his administrative assistant, to pack his suitcase for him while he lounged in bed with a mistress in attendance in the next room. "Get out of that job," was the succinct parental message. At the same time, every worker has to come to terms with situations that are less than ideal. Whatever one's age, a person finds it difficult trying to discern prudently when to accommodate and when to quit or change jobs. Is it time to "hang tough," or move on.

As a parent watches a young adult at work it can become apparent that the work or career that he or she has chosen is not compatible with the individual's capabilities or talents. While these are difficult judgments to make, I think a parent after reflection should offer these observations to an adult child, just as one would to a valued colleague. But offering unsolicited advice in a tactful manner is different from trying to exercise control over a young adult's career. The days of patriarchal family control are gone.

I know of a self-made professional who refuses to speak to his son who chooses to work as a skilled carpenter instead of going into a professional career with higher status. This is an extreme example of parental egoism. Career advice today has to be tentative to be effective. Loving support, perhaps even economic backing for upgrading jobs may be advisable, but authoritarian commands are doomed. Careers cannot be vicariously pursued.

Can a parent help a son or daughter in day-to-day work? Surely some knowledge, or contacts or connections that a parent has, can sometimes be used in a child's work life. Parents can give job leads to adult children. Much work-related information can be passed on in the family as was the custom in traditional guilds when sons followed their parents into the same occupation. Even today when education and specialization may make a parent's fund of occupational knowledge obsolete, parents can know a lot about the dull mechanics of working life in an industrialized society—things such as benefits, pension plans, and tax returns.

And they can know the importance of moving on or seeking to move up in a career.

The question of parents' using direct personal influence to further their children's career is an interesting ethical issue. In earlier days, formidable mothers like Jennie Churchill and Mrs. Douglas MacArthur lobbied all their social connections to help their son's careers. Today, only some discreet plugging of one's children's talents seems appropriate. As long as there is a genuine autonomy on the offspring's part, parents should be able to make some subtle moves to help a deserving and competent offspring. After all, one would help a young friend or protégé. As long as one doesn't overdo it. The pushy stage mother, politico father or monied parent can earn enemies and ill will for a young adult.

After one's child is launched in some work enterprise an interesting new role appears in a parent's life — mother or father of the employee or young professional. "I didn't know how to act when I met my son's boss," said one father. "It was an awkward new situation for me." This powerful successful father was confident when meeting his fellow professionals or clients, but he wanted to be supportive of his son. He didn't want to give any negative impressions by too much parental boosterism, or by letting drop any inadvertent information. Obviously, recounting childhood exploits, or detailing earlier disasters are not appropriate! Here again it may take some adjustment to learn to play the supporting role after having been the star. Giving up center stage means that a parent has to take care not to compete with either the young worker or with his or her employer.

New Satisfactions

With all the new difficulties of launching adult children into careers there are also new satisfactions in store. One of the greatest happinesses in a parent's life can be to work with an adult child in a cooperative enterprise. In the past many children worked with a parent in the family's farm or business, but today the satisfactions of working together are more infrequent and thereby more gratifying. How few firms and businesses can add the "& Sons" to the stationery! Nor do we see "& Daughter" on the office door. Mothers and daughters have had more chance to work together in the home, at least during the cooking involved in family celebrations or when new babies arrive. What may be new is that today mothers and daughters may share experiences as they both work outside the home in jobs and in professions.

Professional mother-daughter collaboration is more unique. One mother who is a professor of philosophy expressed her joy in going to a professional conference and giving a paper with her daughter, a lawyer working in the same field. This experience of being a professional colleague with her daughter was an unexpected pleasure of mid-life. Another professional mother who is a theater director spoke of her delight in working with her daughter, a fine actress. Women who can now more easily enter new fields of work can enjoy seeing their daughters accompany them in their own achievements.

Of course the sharing of professional work can also induce new arenas of conflict. The mother who is a theater director faced a conflict, for instance, when auditioning her daughter for a part in a play she was directing. The mother regretfully had to reject her actress daughter whom she deemed inappropriate for the part. Once this mother had made her professional commitment to direct, the commitment had to supersede her maternal interests in furthering her child's career — but it was a difficult moment. Women, unlike men, are not so inured to keeping their roles as professionals separate from their private lives. The role of father has been traditionally imbued with the aura of impartial judge, but the role of mother traditionally promises unconditional support whenever and whatever. New roles take some getting used to.

The challenge to the parent-child relationship presented by the world of work is not easy. Parents struggle to give nurturing love and unstinting care to their sons and daughters, while at the same time raising them to be hardy enough to meet the outside world's impersonal and critical standards. Partiality must not allow a parent to forget the fact that impartial scrutiny is coming in the larger world of work and achievement.

When all goes well a child becomes a good worker and finds good work that suits his or her capacities and talents. Watching a child have a happy productive work life is one of the great delights of parenthood. If a parent is always to some extent empathetically reliving the stages in the life cycle as their children age, a child finding good work renews a parent's own sense of achievement. Their success is our success. One part of the American dream has come true.

CHAPTER FIVE

Surviving the Sexual Revolution

Dealing with the New Permissiveness and the Old Constraints

A recent *New Yorker* cartoon shows a father and his adult daughter at lunch. The daughter is remarking with great earnestness, "Of course, Dad, when you were young, sex wasn't invented yet." How blind can the young be? Middle-aged parents continue to be sexual beings and sex and gender are eternally agitating realities, whatever one's age and whatever the times. This being so, sexual issues have never passed unnoticed in a family of individuals living together. But much has changed in the last decades; the much heralded sexual revolution occurred. In the last thirty years we have seen an increase in sexual permissiveness as well as more openness in public talk about sexuality. Parents can find themselves strangers in a sexual landscape that their adult children take for granted.

Many middle-aged individuals, like myself, were raised in an environment where sex remained a tabu topic in polite conversation. I can still remember my mother's crimson blush and embarrassed consternation when I asked her what that F——— word meant that I had seen scrawled on a sidewalk. Later, even my scientifically sex-educating father told me to look in the dictionary if I wanted to find out what "fornication" meant. But in a determined effort to be modern, by the second grade my father had apprised me of all the facts (including contraception), and told me that sex was healthy and good. But since the existence of sexual desires and feelings had been left out of the picture, I still could not get a grasp of the mysterious tabus and powers that sexuality seemed to induce. Nothing was explained by my avid reading of the "How to educate your child about sex," book which was hidden in the downstairs bureau drawer.

Later I realized that a sexual double standard was in force in many nonreligious families like mine. Men could be sexually experienced at marriage and allowed to philander occasionally thereafter, but good women must be chaste and faithful. But we also had religious relatives back home in the South, so I knew that in other families a single sexual standard for both men and women was required — men too were expected to exercise self-control. (According to some historians Christianity's demand for a single standard of sexual behavior makes its sexual ethic unique, even if it was more honored in the breach.)

In the privileged schools I attended I encountered a few upper-class girls whose sexual permissiveness seemed to imitate that of the roaring twenties. A few finishing school compatriots regularly slept with their midshipmen boyfriends when they visited Annapolis or went to football games. These affluent young persons did not abide by the sexual restraints of the middle classes, but they did keep their Bohemian sexual behavior hidden and private, much like the Edwardians seemed to do. Their parents too were rumored to be "fast" and prone to affairs. But this group was a minority disapproved of by others.

In this mixed sexual scene there was some confusion about how far a good girl could go and retain her respectability. My father, not so scientifically enlightened that he had given up his Southern ideas of the virtuous lady, instructed me not to kiss anyone until I was engaged. At the time, this Victorian advice did not seem strange or impossible, because these same sexual standards were those of the heroines in my favorite writers, Jane Austen, Charlotte Brontë and Louisa May Alcott. Jane Eyre, Elizabeth Bennet, Jo March and company, were "role models" for young girls, although we didn't know this term. Ideally, a young woman

should be intelligent, independent, feisty, principled, romantic —
and chaste before marriage. Such behavior, we believed, would
lead to romantic sexual fulfillment in a happy faithful marriage.

As for homosexuality, incest, date rape, sexual harassment, pedophilia, and other sexual concerns of the present, such things
were more or less invisible and unthinkable. Divorce was around,
but was exceptional and deeply regretted as a social failure.
Women's liberation and a demand for men and women's equality
at home and work was unheard of as well, although many proto-
feminists like myself held independent ideas and big ambitions.

In the 1960s and 1970s the postwar sexual and social system
began to unravel. A new cultural era appeared in which sex became much more socially salient and explicit; with the advent
of the flower children and hippies an exaggerated sexual permissiveness was proclaimed. Who among us raised in the fifties could
have imagined the public career of Mick Jagger, or Prince, or War-
ren Beatty? It's a long cultural trek from the world of Little Women
to the world of Madonna. Bridging the divide and troubled waters that the sexual revolution opened between the generations
has not always been easy.

But even without a generational shift in sexual ideology it is
not an easy thing to talk to one's children about sexuality. For
one thing, the social tabu against open discussion of one's own
private sexual experiences retains its force in ordinary daily life.
While *sex, sex, sex* may be in every magazine, in every movie,
in song lyrics, and the topic of books, jokes, and media reports,
there is a difference between *general* discussions of sex and specific personal revelations. Most Americans are still determined to
keep their intimate sexual experiences private. Those who break
the convention against public sexual confession, for instance on
TV, may have attention riveted upon their performance, but few
ordinary folks are willing to open their bedroom doors to the
world.

When you value your sexual privacy, sexual discussions and
the giving of sexual opinions are inhibited. There are also cultural constraints against making negative public moral judgments
about the sexual behavior of others. God forbid that we should

sound like sexual prudes or puritans. Sexual discussions or revelations between parents and children are affected by all of the above strictures along with others that operate in family life.

While responsible parents will have taken seriously their role as sex-educators and moral guides for young children, by the time children reach adulthood these sex-education conversations have been left behind. And, if the findings of widespread ignorance of sexual information are accurate, many parents have failed in their duty to give sexual education to their children. Even if ignorant of facts, today's young adults will have been exposed to more public expressions of more varieties of sexual experiences than their parents. Nothing is left in the closet. The latest round of publicity for pedophilia, sex abuse, and incest survivors, for instance, has broken one of the last barriers against open sexual discussions.

With these disclosures of the emotional toll of abuse the society has come to more fully appreciate why it is important that strong incest tabus continue to prohibit cross-generational sexuality within the family. But maintaining a strong incest tabu also inhibits any potentially provocative sexual communication in family conversations. A respect for privacy and restraints on sexual disclosures helps to draw lines between the generations and works to keep sexual boundaries intact.

Clear boundaries between the generations are necessary in early childhood for all sorts of reasons. When parental authority is exercised properly, the parents must clearly be differentiated as the parents, who are sexually bonded and allied with each other, and the children must clearly be seen as the children, whom adults are charged to protect, guide, and nurture. Small children can not be equal friends with their parents; nor is it good for a child to form an alliance, romantic or otherwise, with one parent against the other.

Family therapists have warned us all of intergenerational coalitions in which a child is robbed of childhood by being turned into a substitute spouse, or best friend, or even worse, a substitute parent. We hear terms like the "spousal child," the "parentified child," the "best buddy child" in warnings against blurring generational boundaries in the family system. Tabus on intergenerational sexual discussion or intimate revelations let children remain children.

This strong need for sexual privacy and boundaries between the generations inevitably lingers on into the later relationship of parents and their adult children. Establishing sexual privacy as an adult is one of the ways of separating from one's parents and creating one's independent life. A father in a short story who passes by his son and girlfriend's bedroom is described as reacting "in shame and panic," when he realizes that he is accidentally overhearing their sexual encounter. He then thinks how "a father is repelled at the idea of listening to his son have sex. . . . " This reaction of embarrassment at unknowingly intruding upon an adult child's sexuality seems appropriate in our society.

Even so, one of the things they never mention in the baby books on parenting is how important it will be to have raised a sexually competent adult. The subtle challenge is whether a parent can pass on a positive and healthy attitude toward sexuality that will bear fruit in good adult sexual functioning. All parents can hope that they have raised a child who is a good lover and capable of giving and receiving sexual fulfillment. But because of the mutual need for sexual privacy parents should not seek to pry. I know of a mother who engages in long explicit postmortems with her grown daughters over their previous night's dating and sexual intimacies. This is a pathetic case of blurring the boundaries between generations — as well as an example of voyeurism.

Sexual intimacy with a partner in our culture flourishes within the security of confidentiality. Publicly revealing specific sexual experiences with a partner has been seen as a betrayal of trust and a derogation of the intimacy involved. Males who kiss and tell, describing sexual details of an encounter are seen as degrading their partners, and the same can be said of women when they are equally callous. Inhibition of speech about personal sexuality may be natural and necessary for personal integrity — and especially between parents and children.

Another factor operating in general intergenerational dialogues on sexual topics is the need to negotiate any ideological differences on sexual morality. If parents and children disagree there can be conflict. I say "if," because I have known parents who welcomed the new sexual permissiveness and found themselves in accord with all aspects of the sixties sexual revolution. They felt that the old ways were repressive and hypocritical and inflicted sexual damage on young people and adults. In our liberal New York suburban town some experiments in "open marriage" were played out in the sixties by younger married couples. (This phase did not last long because no one could sustain both openness and marriage; emotional chaos and divorces ensued.) Other parents under the influence of new cultural winds began welcoming their adolescent children's sexual partners to spend the night and have sex at home. Contraception for girls had been provided by the family doctor and this open approach to sex was considered safer and healthier all around. Contraception failure would be handled by abortion, but the hope was that parental openness and approval of what was "inevitable," and "natural," would produce responsible sex. Good sex was considered more a matter of hygiene, psychological health, sport, or aesthetics, and only secondarily a moral or religious matter. There was no generational difference of sexual ideology in these families.

More rarely, parents and children on the conservative end of the ideological spectrum also agree in their sexual attitudes. Together they repudiate the sexual revolution as immoral. These adult children agree with their tradition-minded parents in endorsing premarital chastity and marital fidelity. To carry off this stance there has to be strong support from a local community or a religious group to which children and parents both belong. The Amish, for example, or orthodox Jewish groups in Brooklyn, establish segregated communities and regularly succeed in enlisting their young people in countercultural sexual attitudes.

But what happens when there are differences between the generations over sexual morality? In some unusual cases sexually permissive parents will produce sexually conservative adult children. Parents who matured in a sexually permissive period, say in either the roaring twenties or the unbound sixties, may be surprised by children who reject their parents' sexual freedom.

The children may have watched the toll on the family that permissiveness produced and decided to live differently. Or they may just be generally rebellious like their parents, but now swing in opposition to the right and conservatism. In the same way many adult children of alcoholics become teetotalers and their children become alcoholics.

Religious conversions in adult children can sometimes produce a stricter sexual morality than the more relaxed family tradition. When parents are the more permissive generation, they may feel irritated by the implicit disapproval of their children's following such a straight and narrow path. Permissive parents may disparage their children as "goody goody's" and puritans. Yet the parents of chaste children should count their blessings; they do not have to worry about the harmful consequences brought on by the sexual permissiveness abroad in the land, unpleasant realities like venereal diseases, AIDS, abortions, and grandchildren born outside of marriage. There are by now 200,000 deaths from AIDS, with many more expected. Twelve million cases of other sexually transmitted diseases are reported each year, and 1.4 million abortions are performed annually.

Given the ever increasing sexual permissiveness of our society the more usual sources of parent-child conflict spring from parents adhering to a more traditional moral sexual standard than their adult children do. Conflicts over sexual morality can range from parents who are deeply disappointed and abhor their adult children's sexual behavior to milder differences that can be tolerated and more easily negotiated. An adult child, for example, who is promiscuous is more disturbing to traditional parents than a child who engages in monogamous premarital cohabitation. The practice of living together is becoming a widespread custom and approximates some of the positive goods of marriage.

One can argue that serial monogamy in and out of marriage is the reigning sexual ethic of the majority of Americans. Adultery and casual sleeping around with a multitude of partners are not generally approved of — even for males. Recreational sex may exist in some circles but it is not the rule in the general population. Clearly sex, like any other important human activity, can also be morally misused and abused. Three-fourths of the respondents in one national survey say they consider extra-marital sexuality always to be wrong. Only 1.5 percent of respondents of married persons report that they have engaged in extramarital sex in the year before being questioned. Ironically, individuals may believe that other married people are less faithful than they themselves are.

Premarital sexual behavior at younger and younger ages does seem to have increased, especially among women. Yet, there remain remnants of the culture's sexual double standard in the fact that female promiscuity is still more stigmatized than that of males. Sleeping your way to the top is also morally criticized; and it is considered unacceptable to exploit power or exert coercion in sexual matters. Narcissistic, exploitative, or coercive sexual behavior is not generally accepted in contemporary society — although it still happens.

Parents can be distressed if they observe their young attractive male or female offspring exploiting their sexual partners. One mother and father were deeply disappointed because they felt their handsome and sexy son was little better than a gigolo. He lived off of a series of adoring girlfriends without committing himself to them in more than the most minimal fashion. Another mother was upset that her daughter had two lovers in two different cities, one at home and one in graduate school. A monogamous parent can be scandalized by a son's infidelity to his current live-in lover even if the couple is not married. Once married, an adult child's adultery can create moral indignation and disappointment. Moral disapproval of sexual manipulation, exploitation or expediency can hardly be avoided in certain family situations.

Coping with Conflicting Sexual Moralities

Circumstances make a difference in how an intergenerational conflict plays itself out. Nothing much need be done by a parent if grown children who are unmarried support themselves, rent their own quarters and confine their sexual behavior to their own space. Conversations about conflicting sexual moralities will probably ensue and can follow the good friend test described in the chapter on talking with adult children. Constantly nagging adult children to reform morally, settle down, or get married will not do any more good than nagging them about anything else.

Unmarried grown children living at home present another problem. Whose sexual standards should govern the household? One mother disapproved of her son's sexual behavior and told him that she did not intend to have her house used as a motel. Part of the deal for his living in her home had to be conformity to her moral standards; i.e., casual sex with different partners was not acceptable. Indeed sex with a regular girlfriend would not be allowed in her house.

I believe that this mother and parents who set limits for adult children living with them in a family situation are correct, as I have said before and say again here. Parents have reared children and worked hard to create a home. For years they have paid the rent or the mortgage, bought the groceries, and made innumerable other sacrifices of time and desire to found the family and keep it going. Their efforts have been guided by their own commitments to their beliefs and morally acceptable standards of behavior. Parents have earned the right to determine what sexual norms will operate within their own home. Otherwise parents are being forced to cooperate and implicitly condone or enable ongoing behavior and practices that they find morally offensive.

But what is going to be defined as morally offensive? Parental judgments of some sexual behavior as seriously wrong may be different from their judgments of other sexual practices as wrong but morally tolerable. Some situations with grown children present parents with perplexing gray areas. Many, many adults are now living together for long periods, even for years, without getting married. A third of American women report they have lived together before marriage. When a couple who are living together come to visit, what should parents do? If they believe adamantly that sex and marriage should always go together, they give all their unmarried guests separate bedrooms. Parents who have younger children still at home are often committed to this solution. As one mother said, "It would be a lie to treat them as though they were married when they are not."

This strategy may cause embarrassment but more often the separate room is politely accepted and who knows what happens in the privacy that has been extended? Few parents would go so far as to monitor the sexual behavior of adults who are visiting in their home.

But with adult children who are a long-standing couple living together for years in their own common household, the separate bedroom solution seems rather artificial after a while. One set of parents I know who still believe strongly that sex and marriage should go together finally worked out a compromise with their unmarried adult children who did not share their views. When their grown children have established stable households with long-term committed partners, these parents reason that their children are involved in the equivalent of a common-law marriage. If the sexual partnership is monogamous, the parents treat their adult child's established relationship as a quasi-marriage and the partner as a quasi-in-law. The long-term sexual partner is hard to describe, a "significant other," a "constant companion," a "would-be-in-law?" The partners come for Christmas and family events and are recognized as different from dates or new sexual relationships that have not stood the test of time.

As everyone watching the plethora of unmarried couples living together can see, some of these long-term relationships make it to a legal, public marriage, and some do not. When they don't, there can be a great deal of emotional carnage in the break-up. A nondivorce from a nonmarriage seems as traumatic as the real thing. Parents often are called upon for emotional support in these cases and can have many ambivalent feelings. (Sometimes of course there is only relief that this particular relationship is over!) More often, parents can feel empathy for their child and his or her ex-partner. It can be sad to lose a young person whom parents have grown to cherish. Some odd relationships can continue to exist although there is no word to define them — my young friend is my ex-would-be-in-law, or my adult child's ex-significant other?

There are many serious failings in our current sexual practice. I am one of those parents brought up under the old dispensation who see the new liberties as by no means liberating to the young. Sexual permissiveness is too often psychologically and socially debilitating — especially for women who wish to marry and have children. Women's biological clock ticks away; a long sexual relationship that does not make it to a permanent commitment and marriage robs her of precious time and opportunities. All the while, she, more than her partner, is under the strain of avoiding an unintended pregnancy and if it occurs she may get an abortion, with or without the knowledge of her boyfriend.

Since young persons do not get into and out of sexual relationships with the same amount of willingness at the same time, people get hurt and feel sexually exploited. After several long-term sexual relationships that do not work out, young adults can seem burned out, emotionally exhausted, distrustful of love, and unwilling to make a commitment to marry. Parents are dismayed by the fact that many of their adult children do not marry or marry so late, but the main lesson sexual permissiveness seems to teach is that since relationships do not last, one needs to be wary.

The high divorce rate reinforces a sense of distrust. This hesitation to commit one's self to anyone or to any long-term common future can erode a relationship and make it tenuous. The same sexual and social dynamics work to increase the divorce rates. Parents can observe the sad state of things, but still have little influence over their adult children's sexual behavior. Young persons face enormous pressures to conform to permissive standards. Rumor has it that some changes may be taking place now that AIDS makes sexual permissiveness more dangerous, but change does not seem noticeable yet. Sex is now a life and death decision but society does not give this message.

Easy divorce seems to be undergoing cultural reconsiderations because of the newly publicized negative effects that divorce is found to have on children. But high rates of divorce persist and may go higher according to some experts. Marital fidelity may remain as our operative ideal, but it is hard to maintain in the midst of pervasive sexual permissiveness and a world with crumbling commitments. Being free to live with prospective partners before marriage does not seem to increase the chances for marital success.

Choosing Mates and Getting Married

But young people still get married, sooner or later. As young adults go about choosing mates, parents are basically bystanders. We no longer sanction arranged marriages, although people still try to strive to settle in good neighborhoods and send their children to good schools so that they can meet suitable people from a similar social environment. Parents can hardly be indifferent to the momentous consequences of an adult child's choice of a mate.

A new in-law may be a part of the family circle permanently. When you are old and ill your in-law will have a say in how often you are visited, or perhaps partly determine where you live. Your child's mate will be the parent of your grandchildren. A son-in-law or daughter-in-law will have the power to hurt or help your daughter or son more than anyone else in the world. Will they be a faithful good spouse so that the new marriage will be happy and can avoid the disaster of divorce? This intense concern over a potential marriage partner produces a question about how parents should behave if they are on the scene as a relationship progresses.

Some parents will take the completely hands-off approach. Adults must choose their own marital partners, they think, and no one else has any business interfering in the slightest way. After all, how can any third party ever know what goes on in a relationship? If my adult child chooses a person to marry and seems content, who am I to say a word? No matter what reservations I might have, or no matter how eager I am to secure this potential partner as a member of my family, no word of advice will be forthcoming.

Part of the rationale for this detached stance is the fear that if one offers a negative critical opinion on a proposed partner, one's adult child will blame you for interfering. And if the adult child goes on to marry a mate whom a parent has criticized, the new in-law may be resentful and take one's child out of the family orbit. As one mother put the argument for silence, "I've known too many people who lost their children because of things they said." Disapproving parents may not be received easily in the new household. I know a woman who rarely gets to see her adult son because she criticized her daughter-in-law before the wedding. Her disapproval of the match has never been forgotten or forgiven.

Other parents brush off the fear of future consequences because, as they say, they could never achieve detachment or self-disciplined silence anyway. These parents would speak up if they had serious reservations about the suitability of a potential spouse. After all, parents know their own children well, and often get a good long look at the intended spouse and the couple's relationship. If there are obvious problems, parents — like any other close friends — can feel that they could never forgive themselves for not voicing their observations and reservations, before a final commitment is made. If the adult child has inner doubts, perhaps the parent's opinion will corroborate them and help avoid a serious mistake. While some adult children might resent criticism, other adult children might in the future regret that a parent had been silent at a critical juncture, especially if an unhappy marriage or bitter divorce ensues.

In talkative, expressive, high-voltage families almost all reactions will be expressed, and if conflicts and arguments arise, so what? These families usually have a high tolerance for conflict anyway. Such a parent cannot imagine holding back and not expressing doubts and criticisms. If they put their adult children through the wringer on this decision, it is nothing new. In these kinds of volatile families, the chips will fall where they may, and every opinion will be voiced.

I vote for a middle course between hot and cool strategies. If I had reservations I first would decide whether speaking up would do any good. Will it, perhaps, do harm? After all, it is not unknown for young people to marry in order to prove their parents' opposition wrong — the so-called Romeo and Juliet effect. Any criticisms presented may make the partner seem more valued and defended as all the more precious.

In treading between complete detachment and the no-holds-barred approach I would try to bring up my critical reactions in a tactful indirect way that could not permanently alienate my child. Using the good friends test described in my discussion of communication, I would treat my child with all the delicacy and tact that I would use with a good friend. Since the emotional stakes are higher I would try to be even more shrewd and subtle in my approach. A parent can first make it clear that the young adult's choice is respected and that a parent will be supportive no matter what happens. But then the questions and doubts a parent has can be voiced in a concerned but rather tentative way. Tentative is important both as a strategy and out of honesty. After all, every parent knows of many successful marriages that were originally opposed by everyone, including the couple's parents and friends. Inauspicious differences in age, religion, class, race, ethnicity, and temperament have been overcome. At the same time it is more usually the case that young people going against their parents' considered judgments make mistakes. Knowing both of these things can move a parent to speak up, but to speak up in a delicate, noninfallible mode. If the marriage does take place the parent wants to remain friends.

Once an adult child is married, it seems clear that parents should offer support, or at least not work against the relationship. Marriage is hard enough to make a go of without outsiders, especially in-laws, interfering. Most parents will rightly try to stay out of their children's marriages, while welcoming their in-laws and treating them as though they were their own kin. Contrary to popular report, and mother-in-law jokes, there are many, many happy in-law relationships, more perhaps, than those that are conflicted. In the Bible, Ruth and Naomi were devoted daughter-in-law and mother-in-law, and love for in-laws still blossoms

Good parents work for peaceful family relationships by applying the golden rule to their married children. They treat them as they would want to be treated in similar situations. (Anyone who ever suffered with difficult in-laws knows exactly what not to do.) One ought to criticize only when it is necessary for the well-being of the other and always make an effort to give support, sympathy, praise, and help whenever it is possible.

When an adult child is happily married to a compatible person, there is an expansion of family happiness. There are few descriptions of the deep satisfactions that parents take in the good marriages of their children. Today many parents of grown children remain youthful and active, so it is not unusual to have family visits and outings of the older and younger couple that give great pleasure. As one mother of a grown married daughter remarked, she had never "expected to have so much fun socially with her daughter and son-in-law. It is almost like double-dating when we go out together." When in-laws are as compatible as friends would be, there is companionableness as well as the extra commitment and joy of being kin. These parents can rejoice in the new generation of their family and in the company they keep. They can also be fearful of divorce.

Divorce

Divorce is a fact of family life. The divorce rate has doubled since 1965 and in 1990 1,175,000 couples were divorced. Parents of adult children get divorced and their adult children get divorced. Both kinds of divorces (ours and theirs) create emotional turmoil in a family. Each divorce is the dissolution and breakdown of a small civilization with reverberations throughout the social networks of the couple.

When mature middle-aged parents divorce they can try to ease the burden on their children by not impugning their partner, or forcing children to choose between them. The children may do so anyway and find it hard to forgive the parent they deem most at fault. Divorce always means a marriage has failed, and the marital failure casts a gloom over adult children's lives. Successful mating seems that much more risky for themselves. And divorce adds burdens. Even in the friendliest divorce, adult children now have parents to worry over who do not have support from each other.

In a frequently seen divorce scenario a middle-aged father starts over with a younger wife and the middle-aged mother lives alone. Adult children may then have to give more support to their mother and try to accommodate to a father's new family — sometimes to half-brothers and sisters young enough to be their own children. Divorcing parents of adult children should try to limit the pain of family readjustments even if they are suffering themselves.

Almost all of the advice in how-to-divorce books given to help young children cope with divorce will apply to adult children. Communication, honesty, absolving the children from responsibility and so on, are obvious strategies. A divorcing parent at any age does well to stress to the children that parental commitments continue, no matter what happens next. Whatever new sexual partners, stepfamilies, or half-siblings may be in the cards, loyalty, love, and attention will still be devoted to one's adult children — and their children. There should be a real desire to heal old wounds and, wherever possible, reduce bitterness and alienation.

Practical cooperation will take the form of not making a fuss at weddings, baptisms, funerals, and all the other family occasions where divorced parents have to meet. How many tense weddings have we all now experienced with divorced parents in attendance! Fragmented families have to work at creating new binding ties and alliances. If feuds over money, morality, or property do not enter the picture, people do sometimes seem to be able to accomplish a degree of civility. A whole subspecialty of family counseling has been set up to help postdivorce singles, and to help stepfamilies or reconstituted families adjust. It isn't easy to blend your children, my children, and perhaps our children, into a coherent whole.

There has been less written about how parents of adult children can cope with their children's divorces. In the same way that happy marriages of their adult children increase their parents' happiness, divorce produces distress and sorrow. One mother reported that her son's divorce was the hardest thing she had ever gone through in her life. Her daughter-in-law's mother was dead but before she died the mother had promised her dying in-law that she would take care of her daughter as though she was her own. But she couldn't. There was no way to avert the breakdown of the marriage or the suffering her son and three grandchildren underwent. Her pain is not unusual. Other parents regularly record how excruciating it is to go through a child's divorce.

The helplessness of parents to bring any solution to destructive family conflicts creates extraordinary stress and sadness. Parents wonder if they could have done anything different to have helped avoid the divorce. Almost always the answer is no, nothing.

Today no parent has the control that Franklin Delano Roosevelt's strong-minded and wealthy mother, Sarah Delano, possessed. She is reported to have threatened to cut off FDR's allowance if he divorced Eleanor in order to marry his amour. Divorce would have been the end of his political career as well. Eleanor, who was devastated by the betrayal of her husband's affair, left the divorce decision in her husband and mother-in-law's hands — no model for any woman today.

Anyone who has stayed married knows that marriages inevitably go through difficult times. Parents should encourage their children to persevere by pointing out the ups and downs of marital adjustment. To stay married one has to be committed to the partner, and to be committed to permanent family commitments. Most good marriages are made through struggle and conflicted stages of less than perfect accord.

It is upsetting if a parent thinks that an adult child's divorce is undertaken too hastily or for the wrong reasons. As one set of parents described their adult daughter's divorce, it was more a matter of Joan's vaguely wishing to fulfill herself rather than anything that was wrong. She was not sure she wanted to be married to anyone, even to her thoroughly admirable husband (beloved by her parents). Joan had no real complaints, and despite the existence of three small children demanded a separation in order to find herself. After several years of rejection and waiting, her husband gave up and found someone else. A divorce ensued, to the economic, social, and psychological detriment of the children involved. These parents felt that their daughter had been selfish and immature. But what could they do? Nothing, except bind up all the wounds that they could and support everyone concerned to the best of their limited ability.

Nor can anything much be done when one's adult child has been selfishly abandoned by a spouse. The days of duelling or revenge through blood feud are over — although the feelings of grievous injury remain. A parent may be surprised by the angry hate they feel for a person who hurts their child. The injustice can rankle and create bitterness, but parents can only support one's child and try to stem the wounds. As one mother said of her daughter's bitter divorce, "We could only listen; any questions or advice were no use."

As bad as a divorce can be, no parents would want any child of theirs condemned to suffer in a destructive relationship. Spouse abuse or child abuse, in particular, are emergencies that must be stopped. In these and other cases divorce in the family will seem justified and a necessity, perhaps a relief to the injured partner's family. But even when a divorce seems completely justified or is truly mutual, parents can still worry about the consequences for their child and their grandchildren. Will the grandparents be able to keep contact with their grandchildren, or in the case of a daughter, will the parents be able to help their daughter as a single mother?

Once again the problem of how much to help arises. Will I encourage learned helplessness and immature dependence if I help too much? How much is too much? What can I do if my ex-in-law has taken the grandchildren? Diplomatic skills and wisdom are called upon in such complex and messy family break-ups. Here too the ideal of the family one espouses will make a difference. If parents and adult children accept the extended family and joint households, divorced children who come home will present less of a crisis. Those families committed to an interdependent, separate household will encourage their divorcing child's independence and a return to adult functioning after a period of grieving and adjustment. Many parents will support their daughter's household until they can get on their feet. "Thank goodness we had the money to help her," said one mother. "Of course she was proud and it was hard for her to accept money until she finished her degree and got a job."

The statistics on divorced single women and poverty are frightening. But young men can also be emotionally damaged by divorce. Unfortunately having divorcing adult children is becoming more frequent. When parents have adult children whose marriages fail, it is good for them to read books on divorce so they can try to understand the readjustments that will be necessary. Parents can find themselves going through the divorce vicariously, so they should prepare themselves to be knowledgeable resources for their children and grandchildren.

Positive New Developments in the Sexual Scene

Is there any good news in the changing sexual culture of our society? I would count as progress the movement away from past stereotypes of what a true woman or what a real man must be like, or should not be allowed to do. Less rigidity can be liberating to both sexes. Women can now more easily choose to develop their talents for work outside home and family, and men can become more personally involved in nurturing their children. Every maturing person now has new horizons of development

Of course there are some cultural tensions in coming to terms with new mores. It may take some time for parents to get used to "my daughter the policeperson," or "my son the nurse." The fact that women can generally be more assertive and take more sexual initiative will also seem strange for those reared in the old rules of courtship. It is never easy to work out more equal relationships between the sexes. Changes in a society are uneven and reach different groups at different times. What is old hat on the upper West Side in New York City may be news in Nebraska.

Wherever one lives there is a lot of fumbling around and discomfort as gender roles change at work, in courtship, marriage, and family life. The crash course on sexual harassment that American society went through with the Clarence Thomas confirmation hearings opened many eyes to changes in gender expectations in the workplace.

At home there are also positive revolutions in gender expectations that can be observed. Many young adults who make commitments to marriage and family take on more mutual and equal divisions of the work that goes into maintaining a home and raising a family. In more and more cases both partners work outside the home and both partners share maintenance and child rearing at home. Young couples feel freer to work out different arrangements to suit themselves and their circumstances. Parents watching these new marriages can welcome these new patterns of partnership and equality when they strengthen the marriage.

A close look at the hectic quality of the new generation's family living can also produce profound sympathy. So many young adults are in a frantic rat race trying to meet all their conflicting responsibilities. Some young mothers drive themselves to exhaustion trying to be both good workers and good mothers. Surveys also show that more working women than men still do more of the family's domestic work and child care after work on what has been called "the second shift." Many young husbands and fathers, however, pleasantly surprise their parents by their commitment to equality in their marriages and their concern for fatherhood. Young working fathers, locked into demanding jobs and long commutes, worry about their lack of time with their children, the new working father problem.

Yet I have heard parents criticize the domestic demands that a feminist wife puts upon their son. These parents judge that a truly equal participation in domestic arrangements can burden a young father trying to succeed in his career. This is true if an assessment uses the standards of an earlier day when the husband's career always came first. But today women can also help with the financial burden. And a son who is doing his share at home will benefit the children who receive so much of their father's attention. Parents of daughters, I notice, are most approving of helping husbands who do their full share!

The variety of marital arrangements found today makes it imperative to find a partner who is in agreement on how love, work and housework should be balanced in a family. In a time of change there is a new twist to the mating dance. Parents, whatever their own style of marriage, can find their different children making different choices. Some young adults opt for traditional male and female roles and some choose new kinds of two-career arrangements. Parents may confront "my son the new father," or "my son the old-style male" (a.k.a. my son the male chauvinist pig?). A daughter may be "a radical feminist," or "the new traditionalist." Daughters and daughter-in-laws may keep their own name and pursue part, or full-time careers. It can be intriguing to see different styles of life coexisting in the society, even in one family.

Homosexual and Lesbian Children

Another positive new development in our society is the growing acceptance of persons who are homosexual and lesbian in their sexual orientation. Yet it is still the case that most parents who are told or who find out inadvertently that their child is gay will find it unsettling and hard to adjust to this unexpected outcome. Acceptance will be more difficult if parents are not familiar or friendly with any other openly gay persons in their social circle. Regrets and worries would arise, however, no matter how tolerant and sophisticated the parents.

Not being heterosexual means that an adult child will not have the same kind of marriage and family life that parents have known. And the parents of gay persons will not have grandchildren born in families like their own. Worse still, gay people are a minority group in the population who are regularly subjected to covert and overt discrimination and prejudice. Persecution and violent bias crimes are frequent. If a son is homosexual, the fear of

AIDS and a dreadful death is added to the problems of potential social rejection.

Traditional parents also worry that if their adult children cannot marry in the usual way, they may find it more difficult to sustain a nonpromiscuous single life or to find a stable committed loving partnership. A minority of gay men espouse a flamboyant hypersexual life-style as an essential part of homosexuality, although this claim and these promiscuous sexual practices have changed since the AIDS epidemic. Moral reservations over uncommitted sex with many different partners will color some parents' reactions to certain gay and lesbian life-styles. (These parents would also disapprove of their single heterosexual children acting in a promiscuous way.) Parents of gay adults will worry whether a homosexual or lesbian sexual orientation will make it more difficult to be moral, happy, and socially integrated into society.

Other obstacles to acceptance arise if parents belong to an ethnic group, or religion that considers homosexuality immoral, sinful, or sick. It is hard to overcome the conditioning of a lifetime.

The question of "why?" can trigger parental anxiety and guilt. Why did this child grow up to be gay? Was it something that I, or we as a family did, or didn't, do? These questions will appear after it becomes obvious that a child's homosexuality is not just a bisexual phase, or a brief episode. This may not be clear at first. In permissive circles, political ideologies and increasing tolerance and acceptability of bisexuality can produce temporary gay sexual experimentation. But at some point it can become clear to an individual and to his or her parents that a homosexual or lesbian orientation is permanent.

Is permanent the same as irreversible? Yes, in all probability, although whether homosexuality is reversible or not is still debated by some experts. Equally controversial is the related question of what causes homosexuality, or to be more exact the different homosexualities. Numerous conflicting explanations exist, with no consensus in sight. From a parent's point of view, the most troubling explanations offered are those theories that see male homosexuality as a result of some combination of absent or hostile fathers and overinvolved mothers, and lesbian development as the result of cold mothers and rejecting fathers. In other words, negative family dynamics or practices are thought to be the cause of homosexual development. If parents take these explanations as the truth, then they can either feel guilty and/or critical of their inadequate spouse.

Newer theories do not see parental behavior as causing homosexuality. In more biological approaches, family dynamics or later seductions by peers do not cause same-sex sexual orientation. There may be some organic difference in a child that is present at birth, which predisposes or even predetermines later homosexual development. As one mother said of her son's homosexuality, "I used to blame my husband for treating him differently from the other boys, but then I realized that he *was* different, and so more or less asked for different treatment." While this mother has absolved her husband and herself from causing her son's homosexuality, she still suffers from what to her is her religion's misguided attitude toward homosexual activity; and she is afraid of AIDS. She says that her husband found it more difficult to come to terms with their son's homosexuality than she did. It bothered him more.

I don't know whether there is some natural law that leads fathers to be more resistant to their son's homosexuality than mothers will be. But in America there is a great deal of male fear of homosexuality that keeps males wary; it may impede many males from expressing tenderness and physical affection for one another. Male homosexuality is in general less acceptable and less tolerated than lesbianism. This may be because more male homosexuals manifest a flamboyant life-style and so are more noticeable. Or it may be because male homosexuality is more widespread, and is further from acceptable norms of male behavior than lesbians are from female norms. Or perhaps, more cynically, it is because whatever men do is considered more serious and important than what women do.

Do mothers find it more difficult than fathers to accept adult daughters who are lesbians? I doubt it. Many women already receive their main emotional support from women in their lives—from their sisters, friends, and coworkers. And what woman has not had some unpleasant experience with male sexual aggression to help her understand giving up on men? Lesbian responses can seem an exaggerated form of the feelings of love that heterosexual women already share and feel free to express in public. In the nineteenth century female friendships were quite loving and expressed in ardent language, although few were sexual in expression. There were familiar and acceptable "Boston marriages," in which two single women lived together as two sisters might do.

Once it becomes clear that an adult child is gay or lesbian, loving parents can find themselves in a new world. Learning to understand the ins and outs of gay life in America can take time. If the parent-child relationship has been a good one, mutual love and good will can spur a parent on to new understanding and efforts to overcome internalized prejudices. Love and empathy can drive out culturally conditioned distaste, although certain moral principles about sexuality may remain in place. Often other adult children in the family find it easy to accept their gay sibling and can help parents to come to a positive understanding and acceptance of their child. After either a short or long period of adjustment, parents may come to see their child's gay sexuality as just one factor among many in the young adult's personality and social situation.

What happens next depends upon an adult child's choice of life-style. Some gay persons choose to be out of the closet and some do not. Parents ought to respect their child's decision, for he or she has to bear the consequences of public acknowledgment. Other parental responses should also follow the child's lead. One common reaction of many parents is to adapt the hopes they have for heterosexual children to the life of their gay child. In this approximation, a parent hopes that a child can find a loving and committed sexual partnership that is as stable and permanent as marriage.

Those parents who have enjoyed the benefits of stable monogamous marriages will want their gay children to be able to experience intimacy and companionship, as well as to be able to avoid the turmoil and dangers of promiscuity. Religious persons may be able to sustain single and celibate lives but most adults seem to function better with stable life partners. In this accommodating approach, standards and expectations that one will have for heterosexual in-laws, or perhaps we should say quasi-in-laws, will be transposed to a child's gay partner. These partners will also be welcomed into family celebrations. Accepting the homosexual or lesbian partner as part of the family is often the final stage of accepting the fact that one has a child who is gay.

Some parents may go on to engage in advocacy for gay persons in America, but such activism will be rare. Not all gay persons are activists and there are a variety of approaches as to how public and political gays should be. Of course when a homosexual son contracts AIDS and comes home to die, parents face new questions about disclosure. Many parents of AIDS victims feel that in their milieu they must maintain secrecy in order to shield their child and the family. But the fear of social rejection may be the least of the worries in such a serious crisis.

When an adult child gets AIDS the parents can go through many torments. A long journey to a horrible death lies before them. There is something unnatural in losing a child before one's own death. I shall talk more about family sorrows in my chapter on crises and tragedies.

Final Thoughts

Sexuality will be a part of the parent child story in adulthood. Familiar issues over communication and control arise. Delicacy, tact, and walking the fine line between concern and intrusiveness are called for. Sexuality however has particular challenges attached, some perennial and some arising from the sexual revolution in the culture.

Parents remain on the sidelines but they are not emotionally uninvolved in a child's sexual choices. One of the saddest things about being a parent of adult children is watching them go through pain and suffering. Some pain will arise as individuals bear the consequences of mistakes. Sex, pairing off, marrying, separating, and divorcing are activities that can bring much grief. Parents watch and try to be supportive, but they are not in charge of the narrative. No parents can make their children be chaste, sexually competent, sexually fulfilled, married, faithful, or divorced. An adult child should insist on sexual autonomy and privacy in running his or her own sexual life, even if there are intergenerational conflicts over sexual morality. With time such conflicts may subside. Who has not seen young adult children as they edge nearer to middle age, begin to appreciate their parent's point of view?

While autonomy of the next generation is necessary, parents are still affected by the sexual choices of their adult children — and not just those mistaken choices that lead to familial crises. While an adult child's sexual competence in sexual loving is hidden and private, the resulting happiness of adult children who are sexually well-adjusted with loving partners can resonate in the family. Parents can feel fortunate when the subtle and complex process of sexual development seems to have succeeded. One of the best things about sex is that when all goes well, it effectively increases the ratio of happiness to misery in the world — and in individual lives.

CHAPTER SIX

What Price a Grandparent? Responsible Parenthood and New Reproductive Challenges

Parents of adult children are intensely interested in their sons' and daughters' decisions whether or not to have children, but many don't think it is any of their business to inquire, advise, or exert pressure. I agree, although it is no secret that I want to be a grandmother. I want to have this experience for several reasons. Since I found my own children delightful and fascinating in their babyhood and later development, I am fairly certain that their children will resemble them and be equally wonderful to know and love. How can it not be a happiness to have our family circle enlarged? To see our particular family narrative have another chapter will be a renewal of life. As one mother I know said, "I would like to see my children carry on our family's long line of hard-working people." A traditional blessing assures its recipients that they will live to enjoy the sight of your children's children around your table.

In our uprooted society many people had childhoods in which they never had a chance to know their grandparents well. I did not, and like many others, I desire to make up for this loss by having a chance to be a grandparent and give support and love to grandchildren. Of course those who had grandparents they loved may want to imitate them and give back to grandchildren what they were lucky enough to receive. For aging persons who have done everything else, the grandparent role is one of the few new adventures left in life.

If the testimony of other grandparents is to be believed, even unsentimental skeptics find themselves surprised by their instant attachment to a new grandchild. Some formerly resistant grandparents report themselves as besotted in their adoration as those other fond grandparents who carry pictures and display them to one and all. Becoming a grandparent fulfills the last stage of the life cycle, enriching and crowning a lifetime's effort.

There are other motivations for wanting to be a grandparent that focus upon one's adult children. I would hate to think that my grown children are going to miss what I consider to be one of the most important experiences life has to offer. As a concerned mother put it, "I want them to understand what love and nurturing is all about." How sad to think that they might never know the joy of baby care or, for that matter, never have the satisfactions of having grown children of their own. I also would feel depressed to think that I had raised children who were so hyperindividualistic and self-engrossed that they did not want to give of themselves and care for a new generation. Or suppose they wanted children but did not feel competent enough, or brave enough, to risk the lifelong commitment of childbearing? This confessed sense of incompetence and timidity would not be good news. A refusal to have children would also arouse the suspicion that this choice for childlessness reflects some negative judgment on their own childhood, and on their experience of their parents!

While I feel eager for grandchildren, I recognize that there are other parents of adult children who have little interest in the issue. I know one mother of many children with numerous grandchildren who says that she "does not feel particularly connected to her grandchildren." As a young woman she was interested in her own children, but, as in the Christopher Marlowe quote, "that was in another country and besides, the maid is dead." In this woman's mature years she has moved on to other extrafamilial communities and life projects. Parents who voice such detachment seem to be in the minority. In the grandparenting game it is more often a case of "the haves" and "the have-nots." The have-nots are puzzled to have produced a group of extremely reluctant reproducers. There are a lot of eager parents who are waiting with ever waning hope that their adult children will have children.

In an era of contraception and advanced reproductive technology adult children can voluntarily choose childlessness, delay reproduction for years, or reproduce in new and different ways. The whole enterprise of reproduction is a territory full of new choices, dilemmas, and stress undreamed of three decades ago. Parents and their adult children, like everyone else in the society, may wonder by what criteria anyone decides what to do when faced with new decisions regarding infertility, adoption, surrogate pregnancy, contraception, abortion, and a host of new reproductive technologies? Confusion arises over what responsible parenthood entails. Is it responsible, for instance to use new technology to produce a desired baby? Parents of a young couple can become involved in such puzzling questions as their children ask their advice about new reproductive dilemmas.

New Reproductive Challenges and Choices

Four stories heard from mothers of adult daughters illustrate some of the new questions that can arise about the use of modern reproductive techniques. Two of these mothers who were friends of mine reported that their single daughters had sought their advice about becoming artificially inseminated in order to have a child on their own. Since they saw no marriage or permanent sexual partner in the offing, and the biological clock was ticking, why not have a child by themselves with the help of a sperm bank?

One of my friends then asked her adult daughter how she would raise her child while she continued to pursue her career. Her daughter innocently replied that she planned to have *her*, as the grandmother, take care of her baby while she worked. This mother who had just returned to school herself and was struggling to reenter a professional field tartly informed her daughter that she would *not* be available to facilitate her daughter's single motherhood by sperm donation. In private this mother ruefully commented to me that, while she thought her position was correct, she knew that her own mother would have been more generous and provided child care if she had been a single mother.

Maybe so, I said, but since artificial insemination was not an option in an earlier day, and middle-aged women did not then return to school and work, the family situations were not comparable. Besides, we now also know more about family dynamics and know how important having a father is for a child, be it a son or daughter. Support from two caring parents, a mother and a father, makes a child's outlook better in a host of ways, from improved economic status to better chances at secure gender identity, sexual functioning, and moral development. Single mothers and divorced women raising children alone have an economic and psychological struggle on their hands, so why voluntarily plan to bring a child into this difficult situation? Is a woman's desire to have a baby enough of a moral justification to use artificial insemination? I would say no.

Similar considerations dissuaded the daughter of my other friend. Her daughter decided against single motherhood after reflecting on a child's need for a father, as well as the desirability of having the support and involvement of two extended families with both maternal and paternal kin. This intelligent young woman had a promising career, was a feminist, and so did not believe that women could only be fulfilled by childbearing. Having an anonymous sperm donor as the progenitor of her child lost its appeal.

In a third mother's tale, artificial insemination by sperm donor had already taken place and a baby had been born. The baby was born to the lesbian partner of this mother's lesbian daughter. But the mother, a social worker in the Southwest, did not think it a good thing to choose to have babies in such an unusual way to be reared in a lesbian household. While the mother fully accepted the lesbian orientation of her daughter and her activist lesbian circle, she did not approve of lesbian decisions to have children by sperm donation. Lesbians who had children from earlier marriages, children with fathers, were one thing, but initiating third party conceptions by sperm donation seemed wrong. Her own daughter was not the biological mother of the child, but her daughter insisted that her mother accept the designation of grandmother and play this role. This mother did not think such a redefinition of biological kinship was warranted and family conflict ensued.

I know other parents of lesbian children who react differently. When their lesbian children wish to reproduce artificially they acquiesce and give their support. I have heard tell of a tolerant Catholic family who gave a huge party for the baptism of their lesbian daughter's artificially inseminated baby — but this was in San Francisco, and the parents were the biological grandparents of the baby in question. Of course, if lesbian couples take turns having the babies in their families then each set of grandparents would have genetic ties to some of the couple's offspring, although this might not do much to ease their misgivings about having grandchildren raised without a father in a minority subculture. Here again, much as I approve of the choice to have children, I have reservations about using third parties in artificial reproductive strategies in order to meet a woman's desire to bear a child.

All forms of third-party reproduction present ethical difficulties — sperm and egg donations, embryo donations, surrogate mothering of all kinds. These practices are open to abuse by commercialization and exploitation, and at the very least treat persons as though they were commodities. Oddly enough the question of the extended families or the grandparents involved in artificial reproduction has been regularly ignored in public discussions. Did Mary Beth Whitehead's parents approve of her surrogacy contract to be artificially impregnated, bear Mr. Stern's baby and then give it up? Did the parents of both Mr. and Mrs. Stern agree to the artificial procreation and adoption of the baby now known forever as Baby M?

I am interested in this because before the Baby M case created a furor, I received a call from a fourth mother with another unusual story. This distraught mother from Pennsylvania was anguishing over the fact that her adult daughter was offering herself to be a surrogate mother for $10,000 — with her husband's eager consent. This mother was worried because her daughter had undergone two abortions and been hospitalized for depression, and she did not think her daughter psychologically capable of safely going through with a surrogacy arrangement. When she tried to alert the surrogacy brokers at the clinic to her concerns they kept brushing her off with the reply that her daughter was of age and had given consent. In this case the husband, not your ideal son-in-law by any accounting, was eager for the money, and the surrogacy clinic was not interested in investigating psychiatric problems. The testimony of an adult woman's mother did not count and she had no legal case unless, or until, her daughter should break down or commit suicide as a result of her experience.

The mother of this daughter contemplating surrogacy did not approve of pregnancy for money, or making a contract to give away her grandchild. I agree with her view. As a society we should want to encourage altruistic adoptions and rescues of children already conceived and born, but not countenance selling and buying body parts, or conceiving babies to abandon. Buying eggs, sperm, or womb service from a sexual provider commercializes reproduction and encourages parental detachment from the potential offspring that result from the transaction. Today we want to ensure personal responsibility for one's sexual and reproductive powers, and a high level of attachment and commitment to one's potential and actual children. This is important for females and males. Donors are contracting to sell the genetic heritage they received as gifts from their parents. Sperm donors have been reported to have different feelings about their past actions once they have had children of their own and realize that they have other biological offspring out there in the world. (I wonder what the parents of medical student sperm donors think about their sons' decisions to sell sperm?) Will egg donors and their families be able to remain detached from the children produced from their eggs? Should they be encouraged to be so detached? I doubt it.

Those with feminist ideals don't want to make women who are

surrogate mothers into commercialized breeders — poor women and women with greedy mates being too easily exploited for the money being offered. From a family dynamics perspective, it doesn't seem a wise thing to allow third parties in reproduction to produce an asymmetry of biological relationships. As we know from Cinderella to the latest surveys of children in stepfamilies, more problems tend to arise when one parent is biologically related to a child but the other isn't. One of the traditional unifying bonds between marriage partners is their joint parenting of their children to whom they are equally related. Happily, a couple's joint adoption of a child is also a common commitment enacted by two people together, resulting in an equal relationship to their child.

There cannot help but be a difference from the child's point of view in how he or she enters the family. To be adopted is to be rescued by persons who responded to the social emergency of one's biological mother. (And having been adopted does present problems for some adult children in search of their biological roots.) But to be contracted for beforehand, and artificially produced by third-party surrogacy or egg or sperm donation, is to be brought into the world in a manner different from one's parents. The child is less of a gift and more of a manufactured product. There is also confusion and exclusions over extended kinship ties. Secrecy compounds these problems. Whose child am I? The fact that technology allows us to separate genetic parenthood, gestation, and social parenting does not mean that it is a good thing to do so. When such situations arise, as in infertility problems, I think parents should encourage their adult children to adopt, and discourage third-party options for forming a family. Becoming a parent, and a grandparent, may be achieved at too high a price.

Perhaps the most dramatic and bizarre cases of a grandparent's involvement with new reproductive technology and the procreation of grandchildren is the notorious case in which a grandmother was pregnant with her daughter and son-in-law's artificially fertilized twin embryos. The daughter was born without a uterus and her mother volunteered to carry her grandchildren

to term. What about the moral appropriateness of this arrangement? Here there is no intrusion of a genetic third party, just a
third-party gestation by the grandmother who will remain a part
of the children's family. Do most of the moral objections against
third-party reproduction exist in this case? No money is being
exchanged, so this is not a matter of a rich woman exploiting a
poorer woman.

There will be no genetic asymmetry in the family because the
twins will be equally related to both their mother and father. The
extended kinship system will remain intact, for the child will still
have grandparents and kin from both sides. No donor has sold or
given away their procreative heritage in egg and sperm, without
intending to be responsible for the results. Only the grandmother
is being used as a biological provider and womb, a means to an
end — albeit in an altruistic act. Maybe the last reservation would
be enough to create moral, ethical, and legal problems — but
then this is such an exceptional case, how many daughters are
born without a uterus?

Many parents of young adults who are reluctant reproducers
might not resist some ironic observations of this case. How amaz-
ing that this woman was still young enough to be pregnant when
her daughter got married and decided to have children! Many
grandparents-in-waiting think that they will barely be able to tot-
ter around, if and when their adult children finally get around to
marriage and procreation. I think with some dread of my friend
who finally became a grandmother at eighty-four — just before
she died at eighty-six. She had married in her forties and so had
her only son. Other mothers of adults can thoroughly understand
why the grandmother in the surrogacy case was willing to be pregnant for her daughter. It was altruistic, yes, but from a selfish
point of view, if this is what it takes to get grandchildren then
it may be a small price to pay.

Even in a serious mode, I cannot be critical of altruistic grandmother surrogacy in such a rare case of emergency. I am also in
favor of other reproductive technology that is not so exotic, and
does not separate genetic, gestational, and social parenting. Using medical technology and in vitro fertilization to help infertile

couples conceive, gestate, and have their own genetic children is aiding family formation without the intrusion of third parties. Here technology is remedying a couple's medical and social problem. The pain of infertility is relieved without using any other person as a means to an end. There may be ethical problems about medical costs and access to infertility programs, and how to protect any extra embryos produced, but without third-party intrusions I see few psychosocial drawbacks for the child, the couple or the family.

Infertility among young couples seems to be increasing due to a host of reasons. Parents who have infertile children can share the sorrow of their children twice over, once for them and once for their own lack of grandchildren. Supporting one's children through the arduous struggle to overcome infertility may be draining, but when there is success the birth of a child and a grandchild is a joy. If there is medical failure, parents can support their adult children who choose to adopt, another arduous and expensive quest. Those who go the adoptive route have a large selection of literature to guide them through the pitfalls and psychological stress of the adoptive process. The commitment of grandparents to the search and to the new adopted child will help the whole family's adjustment.

It is also possible of course to help one's children come to terms with childlessness. More and more of the population will for various reasons not produce children, and there are many other ways to be fruitful and happy persons outside of child rearing. While I dearly want grandchildren and think procreation is important in life, I also think that the choice of whether to have children or not is up to the prospective parents. Others must respect the choices that are made. While parents might prize having children as the best and happiest way to live, and desire to be grandparents, I do not think it right for them to pressure their adult children to have offspring. Such social pressure is too intrusive and too controlling. Parents of my generation suffered from intrusive comments on our positive reproductive choices, "What! Pregnant again!" and many even more insulting remarks. We learned a lesson about insensitivity.

In fact, delicacy and the desire not to intrude may mean that reproductive options may never get discussed. Parents feel inhibited from bringing up the subject of possible grandchildren unless their children bring it up first. If marriage is the M word, grandchild is the G word that is avoided in sensitive-to-privacy parent-child conversations. As one mother replied to a questioner about whether her adult children were planning another baby, "I don't know. When they tell me I'll tell you." Public discussion seems warranted only when it is a case of producing an heir to the throne, as in Charles and Diana's case. Then everyone can feel free to get into the act and enter discussions about responsible parenthood.

What Is Responsible Parenthood?

Parents of adult children, like everyone else, must confront the ambiguity of the two different meanings of responsible parenthood. In one sense it means successfully meeting or responding to the needs of the children one has. (And in a sense this book is a reflection on how long parenting can continue!) The other meaning of responsible parenthood refers to making wise and prudent decisions about when, whether, and how to become a parent in the first place. Obviously these two meanings are interrelated since the notions one may hold about what it takes to care for children will influence one's decisions about having them.

Most parents who have stayed married, or even remarried people of their own age, will be well out of the childbearing business by the time their adult children are facing these decisions. Only a few middle-aged fathers of adults may have remarried younger women and be facing the question of second-time-around parenthood. They have to decide what their responsibilities are to their new wives, their present adult children, and the new child to be, who as a young adult will have either a dead or a very old father. For the most part, however, parents of adult children think about responsible parenthood in light of their grandchildren to be.

Naturally, parents of adult children have already given a resounding message about parenthood by their own reproductive behavior. Was their own conduct responsible parenthood in both senses of the word? Many parents may feel some misgivings because, in retrospect, they can see they were not terribly self-conscious or reflective about their childbearing decisions. Many parents in the fifties had children, even big families, with the unquestioning assurance that this was best for themselves and for their children. We were energetically committed to being good caretakers, but we did not carefully analyze the reproductive choices we were making. The upbeat spirit of the times was familial and domestic, a trusting optimism that all would be well. In the general confidence of the period, pronatal choices remained unexamined. It was just assumed that young persons got married and produced a family, at the very least, a boy for you and a girl for me.

Conditions for childbearing have changed. I would say that it is about ten times as hard to have a child today as it was in the 1950s, psychologically, economically, and socially. There are more external and internal obstacles. There is, right at the start, the problem of making an overt, explicit decision to become a parent while faced with many different options and life-style choices. Women today do not automatically assume that they will play a domestic role as homemaker and family culture-bearer.

Many women work and others are committed to the careers for which they have been educated and prepared. In economic recessions young couples are often struggling to make it with a working wife's income necessary for the family budget. With a two-job or two-career family, having a child challenges the whole style of life. Who will take care of the child? Worry over the cost of child care and the anxieties over finding reliable adequate caretakers take a toll on parents.

At the same time the cost of health care for pregnancy, delivery, and pediatric care has skyrocketed along with the cost of baby equipment and so on. One mother who had raised a very large family took one look at the complicated modern car seats for babies and allowed as how she could never have afforded or accommodated all the seats she would have needed in one car.

In those days babies and toddlers sat in rickety seats and more or less bounced around in the carpeted backs of station wagons. And expensive car seats are just the beginning of what today's babies seem to need. The average standard of living for a middle-class child seems to have escalated in the last thirty years. Those who speak of "designer children" are referring to the services, lessons, experiences, and equipment that middle-class parents think are basic requirements for child rearing. The complicated scheduling of children's lives is one new task; without siblings or other children around, parents must engineer play dates for children and constantly worry about their safety in getting from place to place.

Must a parent be totally financially secure and able to provide all the frills to responsibly have a child? It seems a requirement that only a Rockefeller or the most affluent young couple could meet. Perhaps a more realistic assessment should be that a parent's commitment to the child, and their present earning capacity and future prospects, are in good enough order to provide an average acceptable environment for their children. If in the present a young family is enduring a time of scarcity, perhaps the prospects for the future are better. A person near to completing some professional training, for instance, has a good economic future.

Another more subtle thing to judge is how much "social capital" a couple has in relation to economic wherewithal. Social capital is made up of cultural intangibles: extended family support, a religious community, educational aspirations, and internalized moral commitments to work and duty. Young parents with good character and social capital who are committed to each other and to their children are going to be responsible caretakers. The resources grandparents are willing to provide in either financial or backup support are also a part of a young couple's social capital.

Having children today is delayed because young parents-to-be seeking economic security for their children as well as other goods often try to have both husband and wife complete their education and training before childbearing. In a time of economic stress, as well as high divorce rates, women feel that they too must be able to earn a living. Few women will stay home and take care of home and children for a lifetime, although contrary to some media reports, most young families do have mothers who stay home while their children are small.

There is even a return to the traditional pattern among many highly educated and affluent women who quit careers for an extended period in order to stay home with their children. They find the strain of trying to pursue a high-powered job along with childbearing and child rearing is too much to endure. When it isn't too financially oppressive to do so, women take time out. Women do not want to miss their children's infancy or worry about whether child care is adequate. Young husbands are also committed to their children, but if one parent is going to stay home it is more often the wife who is more comfortable playing a more traditional nurturing role. House-husband fathers can do a good job, but it is harder for them to swim against the tides of cultural custom.

Parents of adult children can have many positive and negative attitudes toward the young family's decisions about responsible parenthood. Many parents while respectful of their children's privacy and autonomy cannot help but be privately regretful if their children choose childlessness, or that their grandchild is a one and only. Others, on the other hand, can worry that their children are having too many children or having them too soon, or having children that they cannot take care of properly. The issue of selfishness comes up. It may be selfish not to have a child because it threatens the affluent comfort of a narcissistic life-style, or it can be selfish to have children because a person wants to have a baby and doesn't take account of the baby's need to be well taken care of in the future.

Assessing responsible parenthood is a subtle and difficult judgment call. It is the individual couple's decision, but the attitudes of others in the family will also have some influence. We cannot help but affect each other by our values and attitudes. While parents of the young parents-to-be have already given their main message by what they actually did with their own childbearing and family decisions, influential indirect conversations still take place. Parents of grown children reflect upon what they faced and talk to their adult children about their own experiences. Comments on the reproductive behavior of others also convey messages and reveal parental attitudes. Still, direct advice to an adult child is better left undelivered. Personalities, temperament, and social resources differ, as does moral character and the ability to weather risks and difficulties.

Reproductive decisions and child-rearing decisions are inevitably gossiped about, however, in private comments and prudential assessments among intimates. Parents complain to each other, and to a few close friends, about their adult children's decisions. "I think they are waiting too long," says one father about his adult children who are still childless after a decade together. "They seem to be getting so comfortable and set in their ways; can they adjust to the disruption of a child?" Parents can wonder whether a generation of older, dillydallying, and long-delaying couples can make a decision before it is too late. Parental complaints about adult children not having babies are matched by the complaints from a different set of parents about their children having "too many." "Why did they have another child when they knew unemployment was coming?" said one disapproving mother. "They know where babies come from, don't they?" "My daughter is exhausted from having so many children so soon." This latter is a parental lament more common in an earlier day. Many private criticisms and worries come from parents who would not voice these opinions to their adult children.

Other Reproductive Technologies:
Contraception, Prenatal Testing, and Abortion

Contraception is so commonly accepted in American society that there are few disagreements over it. The only dissenters are some orthodox religious groups, so any intergenerational tension over the morality of birth control is often confounded with religious differences. Secular Jewish parents are sometimes worried when their adult children convert to orthodoxy and devote themselves to procreating big families. Some conservative Catholic parents may have differences with their children over the birth control issue as well. But, by and large, either tactful silence or brief spasmodic intergenerational disagreements may be all that occurs over this issue. Responsible use of contraception for family planning seems to be part of our accepted American norm for responsible parenthood. Sterilization after completing a family is also a more or less completely accepted procedure, which parents will not know about or if they do will have no objections.

Abortion, however, is often a less private matter. Many parents of adult children get into this debate when they know about a new pregnancy, or when an adult child consults them about the advisability of abortion. Parental efforts to persuade, and even socially coerce their daughters, can appear on both sides of the issue. I know of a case in the Midwest in which parents threatened that, unless their divorced daughter got an abortion, they would fire her from her job in the family business and cut off financial aid to her and their four-year-old grandson. This woman was pro-choice but her choice in this case was to have her accidentally conceived child that she did not want to abort. Such parental coercion seems intrusive and punitive.

Other pro-choice parents who think abortion for social reasons justified might simply support whatever reason their daughter gave for having an abortion. Some more conservative pro-choice parents might think it right to abort only in emergency hard cases — rape, incest, or genetic disease in the fetus.

Indeed, one of the things that makes childbearing so much more stressful today is the availability of prenatal testing and elective abortion. This combination presents hard choices about taking genetic risks. Often the information about possible risk is ambiguous and inconclusive. These difficult decisions can torture young adults and have repercussions for their parents as well. Of course, attitudes toward abortion influence willingness to undergo various tests. If one does not believe it right to abort even a potentially handicapped child, then it is not critical to find out the state of the fetus if there is no treatment available for a condition. Potential parents with pro-life principles against abortion will face many pressures in a culture that emphasizes health, self-sufficiency, and control of reproduction.

Involuntary pregnancy is a fact of modern life. Many pro-life parents I know have helped a single daughter through an involuntary pregnancy and then helped support their grandchild. Others parents have supported their daughters who choose the painful option of adoption. Since unmarried motherhood is not socially acceptable in most circles, a daughter's unmarried pregnancy can present many economic and psychological hardships for her and her family. Bearing this cost can seem worth it if parents identify with the developing human life as their own grandchild.

But at this point in our society the right to obtain an abortion is virtually unlimited and many young pregnant women, unmarried or married, will choose to abort for different reasons, with different degrees of acceptance or regret. Pro-life parents can experience the sorrow of being a helpless bystander to an abortion in the family. Because another person's privacy is in question, these wounding experiences are almost never spoken of, or openly grieved. Parents can be deeply disappointed by the choices of their adult children that deeply offend their own moral standards.

Many parents have also seen negative aftereffects of abortion in their children's lives with the same sadness and helplessness that they felt about the original abortion decision. Some young women who have abortions suffer psychological aftereffects, a fact that has often not been recognized since other young women do not have such reactions. Investigations into the psychological toll of involuntary miscarriages and stillbirths on women, men, and their families have just begun. When all such losses occur, parents who love their children can only try to understand and support them. Even if there have been moral disagreements about abortion, after an abortion has already taken place it is important to work to see that everyone concerned is healed.

If in an opposite situation, a young couple does not abort when a pro-choice parent thinks it called for, then in this situation also, acceptance should be forthcoming. Usually the presence of a new grandchild will win over disapproving grandparents. Infants have their ways of getting what they need from the surrounding family. Once a pregnancy begins, voluntary or involuntary, parents can be supportive and helpful in many ways. Times of transition and risk are those periods in the life cycle when the extended family can play its buffering role as a supplemental resource to an individual. Kinship groups everywhere rally round to help a new family get started. It is recognized that childbearing and child rearing is an investment in the family's long-term future.

Child Rearing and Grandchildren

Child rearing is an enterprise that every parent has undertaken and to some extent the test of one's own child rearing will be found in watching how one's adult children perform when it is their turn. Did I pass on good values and personal competencies that are going to bear fruit in the third generation? In a crude way, you want your children to give as good as they got, to be as good a parent as you were and maybe even better. It isn't exactly competitive parenting but a desire to have good things happen to those you love most.

Realistically, given human nature, many parents are going to have some criticisms about their adult children's parenting practices. There is an incredibly strong urge to point out shortcomings and give advice. But the best strategy, almost certainly, is to maintain tactful silence until one is asked for advice. Here again is a time for the discipline of the tongue and a determination not to be intrusive or treat an adult as though he or she were a child in need of a stream of instruction. Everyone has a right, as always, to set standards in one's own household, but telling adult children how to raise their children is not going to be welcomed. Unless it is really a serious problem, benign nonintervention works best.

At the same time a parent can offer help, help which doesn't undermine or encourage dependency. For some families there are still strong intact family traditions of how parents should help their children in childbirth and the stressful years afterwards. Mothers may attend births or go to help out when a young mother comes home from the hospital. Other parents routinely provide financial or baby-sitting assistance. For many working mothers child care is provided by grandparents.

Other families improvise or make different rules to fit their own circumstances. As one active professional widow with numerous grandchildren said, "I don't baby sit unless it is an emergency; I am too busy with my own work." But this same grandmother welcomed any of her adult children to come over to visit and bring the grandchildren at any time, as long as they remained in charge of the children. With families who self-consciously are creating new customs as they go along, grandparents can still find many ways to provide help and remain interested and involved.

Today the relationship of grandparents and grandchildren can take different forms. At one extreme, grandparents with a mentally disturbed or drop-out child can be caught in the family tragedy and end up as full-time parents to their grandchildren. The drafting of grandparents as child rearers used to happen because of disease and untimely deaths, but today it is more likely to be caused by addiction and drug use. We see news stories and articles devoted to this turn of affairs, with the arduous difficulties described of aging second-time-around parents learning to cope. At another extreme, many grandparents are cut off from their grandchildren by distance and divorce.

In the middle range of outcomes are the more satisfying family patterns where there is not only love but frequent interaction with grandchildren who are brought up by their own parents. Active involved grandparents can offer another adult voice in the lives of their grandchildren; they can be sympathetic and offer concerned support in all the ups and downs of their grandchildren's lives. More studies of grandparenting and the grandparent relationship are appearing. This happens, ironically, as the relationship becomes more problematical, more self-conscious, and more highly valued.

I have heard many fortunate grandparents express admiration

for how wonderfully well their adult children are tackling the child rearing enterprise. These grandparents are delighted that their adult children are coping so well and have become such good parents. Whatever new combinations of work, careers, and homemaking may exist in the young family, the grandchildren are getting what they need to grow and flourish. Grandparents in these optimal cases are happy; they are renewed by watching their grandchildren enthusiastically meet the world.

CHAPTER SEVEN

Surviving Accidents and Illnesses: The Inevitability of Suffering

"To have a child is to give a hostage to fortune," John F. Kennedy said on the birth of his child, but he did not live long enough to know how true this ancient saying can be. Parents cannot control the future. They cannot guarantee that bad things will not happen to their children. JFK's mother, Rose Kennedy, could offer a better reflection on the ups and downs of the turning wheel of fortune. She had placed a retarded daughter in an institution, had four of her adult children die violent deaths, and lived to see several of her grandchildren come into public disrepute, with one dying of a drug overdose. Parents always and everywhere can suffer sorrow and pain through the unforeseen crises and tragedies in their children's lives.

Consider, for instance, the all-too-frequent automobile accident. Many parents have been through the horrible experience that starts with a telephone call in the middle of the night. In our case the message was, "Your daughter has been in an automobile accident and is in the emergency room asking for you." The fact that she was able to *ask* for us was a hopeful sign, and indeed, after an agonizing, interminable twenty-minute trip to the hospital, we found that her injuries were minor, a broken arm and lacerations. Another set of parents I know had a more grim experience. The telephone call they received conveyed the message that their adult daughter was in the emergency room fighting for her life and in all probability would be dead by the time they got there. While driving back upstate from a visit home, she had been in a head-on collision with a truck.

Then began the dreadful drama of getting to the hospital in a distant city, living through an operating room vigil that finally resulted in a narrow victory over death. Their daughter survived and after six weeks in the hospital, these parents carried their injured daughter home for a six-month rehabilitation process. Daily the parents and the rest of the family provided nursing care. Their daughter fought her way back to health and came out of the gruesome experience a stronger person. These parents who gave so much feel grateful that their child is alive and back to normal.

Nightmare episodes, as with the sudden accident, can be an acute emergency for parents of adult children. In these crises, parents expend enormous energy to cope with the challenge, and after a short or long struggle, the adult child returns to normal life. But some adult children do not recover after an accident or return to full functioning. Head injuries, for instance, may permanently alter intellectual capacities and change former personalities. When a crisis does not pass, when children do not return to normal, the original misfortune becomes a chronic problem that may become a tragedy. Some blows of fate cannot be remedied. Lives are altered forever.

Other kinds of tragedies arise, but not from an external chance event. Tragedies can come about because a child, through flaws of character or inherited vulnerabilities, succumbs to some temptation in a destructive environment. Chronic cases of drug addiction or a mental illness may slowly develop over years — and they bring trouble and sorrow. Parents facing either chronic conditions or sudden crises can suffer terribly, while at the same time they are puzzled over how to respond.

Every middle-aged parent can supply sad stories of crises their friends and relatives have encountered with their adult children, or, closer to home, tragedies that they have experienced themselves. Everything I discuss here has happened to some parent I know personally. Middle-class status no longer offers surety or safe protection for offspring. Automobile accidents occur in all classes, and adult children (or their passengers) are injured, maimed, permanently handicapped, or killed. Other young adults are injured or killed in sports or mountain-climbing accidents. One sad day I attended two funerals of beautiful young men from our town, one killed in an auto crash and one in a mountain-climbing accident.

Diseases, like accidents, can also appear out of the blue to strike down young adults and create emergencies for their parents. Young people have strokes, contract cancer, MS, and other dread diseases, including various forms of mental illness. A young professional woman I know suffers severe disabling complications from Lyme disease. She can no longer work and has returned to her family home. These older parents thought they had launched all of their children, but now find themselves caring for a formerly independent adult — who hates being reduced to the dependent state of an invalid.

AIDS, the ultimate disease, also reduces an adult child to a dependent person in need of family support and care. AIDS may be slowly entering the heterosexual population and can no longer be thought of as only a disease of homosexuals, drug abusers, or those receiving blood transfusions. We all watched Kimberly Bergalis waste away with her parents in loving attendance and there have been a host of other poignant publicized cases. I know of a mother whose wonderfully accomplished adult son was a hemophiliac and died from a tainted blood transfusion. Such a double blow of unjust fortune is doubly hard for a family to bear.

Parents with adult children who have AIDS can know what it was like to live during the epidemics of plague. In some cases, a family is feared and avoided after AIDS strikes and the information becomes public knowledge. There is a special horror in seeing a formerly healthy adult child cut down, destroyed in a hopeless war.

At least when adult children actually join the military and go to war, they have a fighting chance for survival. In a military engagement, some are safe, some wounded, some killed, and some disappear into that torturously ambiguous category, missing in action. Parents find themselves praying for peace with special fervor, when their sons are at a vulnerable age for a draft, or freely join up. Young men, and now young women, can voluntarily expose themselves to violence.

Today in the U.S., of course, there is also violence on the street and at home. Random street muggings or attacks can be a part of life in a city, no matter how affluent the person is. But since crime is higher in bad neighborhoods, parents can often want adult children to live at home rather than in the poor housing they can afford. This is especially true of daughters. Young women are exposed to rape and date rape — as we realize when we are exposed to a publicized trial like the William Kennedy Smith case. (And how horrible for a parent to face the fact that a son could be a rapist, as well as promiscuous!) Other rapes are often kept secret within the family, although still causing pain for the victim as well as her sympathetic family. One mother I know valiantly supported her daughter's recovery after a rape and helped her move from the seedy neighborhood where it had taken place.

Murder, the ultimate act of violence, touches more and more families. I myself know four middle-class parents who have had adult children murdered — two by their friends(?) and two by slight acquaintances. (It is more rare to be murdered by a stranger.) In such cases the wheels of justice can turn so slowly that a parent of a murdered child may live with the agonizing legal repercussions for years. As one sorrowful father commented, "It's been two years now, and the man who killed my son has never spent a night in jail." Recovery from the violent murder of a child is so difficult that support groups for such parents have been formed.

If murder is becoming more common, suicide is virtually an epidemic among young adults. Self-murder has been increasing among the young at alarming rates. Almost every extended family has been touched by the tragedy of a young member ending his or her life in its prime. Almost every parent has a friend whose adult child has committed suicide. Young adults throw their attractive, well-cared-for bodies from high windows, they hang themselves, take drugs, put plastic bags over their heads, and so on. Some young women starve themselves to death. Worst of all, suicide has a destructive ripple effect through peers and near kin. A suicide by one sibling often produces suicide in another. One remembers with horror the philosopher Ludwig Wittgenstein's family in which three of the eight adult siblings killed themselves.

In addition to overt suicides there are all the self-induced deaths from drug overdoses. These drug deaths also can run in families, as those of us can attest who have attended the funerals several years apart of adult siblings who have each overdosed. Sometimes the parents knew of the addiction and had struggled for years to get their children to go into treatment. Sometimes the drug use was hidden. A call from Boston notified one shocked Midwestern mother, "Come and get your daughter, she is a heroin addict and needs hospitalization." When this beautiful, intelligent daughter cleverly succeeded in convincing her mother that she did not need treatment, she joined, within the month, the ranks of young adults who have died from accidental drug overdoses.

Alcoholism is rampant among the young as it is among other age groups. Parents who face alcoholism and other drug addictions are often unprepared and frustrated in their efforts to help their adult children. Watching a beloved child self-destruct while being forced to stand by helplessly is excruciating. Some parents try to deny it is happening for as long as possible. Once denial is overcome it is still no easy thing to get an adult into treatment. Adults must voluntarily choose to be treated if they have not yet broken the law. I say "yet," because prolonged drug use usually leads to legal troubles. Middle-class young persons go to jail because of their use of illegal drugs and their involvements in drug dealing.

Other kinds of crime can also lead to incarceration, with all the suffering that this brings to the young adult and to the parents of the imprisoned. Who, as a middle-class parent, could have been prepared for this? Today, what immigrant parents and ghetto dwellers have long been familiar with, becomes a reality for other parents.

This long litany of crises and tragedies with adult children can be increased when they marry and have children of their own. With unhappy marriages there are problems of the couple's relationship and divorce discussed elsewhere, along with the suffering of infertility and miscarriages. When grandchildren appear, then their diseases, deaths, and disabling handicaps can add to the sorrow of their grandparents. A stillborn baby, or a sudden infant death, or a lingering death of a grandchild can take many years for everyone in the family to overcome. The closer the parents are to their children and grandchildren, the more they will resonate with their losses.

Responding to the trials and tragedies of one's adult children is not easy. The different misfortunes that may appear require different kinds of reactions. Perhaps we can discriminate between what is required in a one-time crisis and emergency as opposed to the challenges presented by long-term and chronic conditions. There is also a difference in one's reaction to external chance events, and those more insidious problems that arise from personal moral failings and free but irresponsible behavior.

Emergencies and Crises

Parents whose children are grown and living away from home can be catapulted into a sudden external misfortune that no one could predict or do anything about beforehand. Such disasters, like an accident or an assault, happen without warning. Something terrible and unforeseen has happened to one's child. Parents are suddenly confronting a family crises. Most horrible, of course, is the grim message that death has already taken place.

Emergencies galvanize parents. They have had a lifetime of parental coping and those who are still middle-aged and vigorous go back into action in the crisis mode. Whatever has to be done will be done. In the sudden deaths of unmarried children, parents arrange funerals and burials. Since very few young persons can imagine that they will ever die, few have made any arrangements or plans. Sudden accident victims get cared for, adult children struck by disease will be helped to the best of the parents' ability.

In what turns out to be a protracted emergency, parents can

find themselves supporting their adult child in a long lingering death — from AIDS or some other lethal disease. At least in a lingering death there is time to demonstrate love, achieve reconciliations, and say good-bye, as there is not in a sudden death.

In other accidents and misfortunes young adult children do not die, even though they have lost consciousness permanently. In these cases parents may have to make painful decisions about continuing treatment when a young adult is in an irreversible coma, physiologically kept alive by modern technology. We have all seen the suffering of Nancy Cruzan's parents, and Nancy Jobes's, and Karen Anne Quinlan's, all caught in the legal morass about what treatments their daughters would have wanted.

Whether to disconnect a machine or withdraw feeding tubes when medical futility has been reached, has become an all too familiar parental dilemma. In my opinion, we should allow the dying to die, once all hope of recovery of any future state of consciousness has been lost. Young adults, like their aging parents, need to voice their wishes, so a family can reject any overuse of medical technology. In a grieving state it is very difficult for parents to make agonizing decisions about allowing death, however inevitable.

Suicide, which is not inevitable, is a more devastating emergency because it usually leaves all family relationships unresolved, and bequeaths a host of torturous questions. Parents are hurt and overwhelmed with thoughts of what might have been. Death in the prime of life is so senseless, so wasteful, so cruel. If some suicides wish to wreak vengeance upon their parents, they succeed. No parent can erase this pain from their mind and heart. Even when a parent is sure that a child loved them and wished them no harm, a child's suicide is a terrible blow. Parental guilt and anxiety can coexist with anger and sorrow.

Guilt appears because parents cannot help but wonder whether they could have done anything to prevent this tragedy. If there was some warning that a child was depressed, parents can torment themselves that they did not act more forcibly. Perhaps they had already urged treatment, or were even paying for it, but parents can still flagellate themselves with the thought that perhaps a different, better treatment for depression or drug abuse might have been procured. One of the grim ironies of suicide is that often a depressed person must be somewhat recuperating before he or she can feel energized enough to be able to carry out the act of self-destruction.

If, on the other hand, a young person showed no outward signs of distress, the puzzle is even more agonizing as to why, why? No caring parent can help feeling emotionally battered. The devastation is traumatic because there can be no more communication and dialogue. The finality of death is oppressive, and as a parent it can seem a particular horror to have your child die before you.

In senseless tragedies of premature death a parent is tempted to rail at the universe. The death of a child is a death of part of one's self, one's past life, one's stake in the future. Any search for a philosophical explanation or religious reason for a tragedy is more or less fruitless. Unfortunately, some parents are broken forever by a child's death. For those willing to fight defeat, the challenge is to meet the crisis, to grieve, to continue on with life — to learn to survive.

After some taxing parental emergency is over, after the crisis has passed, there remains the need for recovery. A frenzy of coping activity may have kept parents from thinking or caring for themselves. But if the rest of life and one's other family relationships are going to flourish, some attempts at healing are necessary. Many parents find solace in groups of parents who have had similar experiences. In an age-old practice, parents find that solidarity and helping others brings balm for one's own sorrow.

American culture is getting more sophisticated about the need for grieving and sorrow, now sometimes called *griefwork*. The older stoic demand that a person should not be weak or emotional is waning. It is now recognized that in order to heal, a parent has to mourn and go through an extended process of reintegrating one's life without the lost child. Many new creative ways have been developed to accomplish the inner process of reconciliation — even when the break with a child was full of unresolved tensions.

One mother of a young, mentally ill son who used drugs and died suddenly in the midst of bitter family quarrels, found solace and healing through imaginatively reworking memories. In this process a parent envisions an earlier time with the child and initiates in imagination a healing dialogue, a positive reworking of what had been stifled, curtailed, or deformed in the past. In the mind's eye, the actual dreadful interchanges and mutual recriminations do not have to be the last word. The imagined conversations reestablish feelings of love and peace; they are a method of healing. In this way, a parent's repetitive, resurgent cycling of agonizing images and distressing questions can be broken. For those who can use the imagination in this re-creative manner, overcoming grief is made easier. Self-help group experiences or individual therapy or use of healing memories may not be for everyone. Healing and recovery can take place in many unique and individual ways. Some parents may take up arms against the cause of their child's tragedy in political campaigns or in other community activity aimed at prevention of similar tragedies. Those who have seen how devastating an event can be for a victim's family may try to organize help for themselves and others in similar straits. A father whose son was in an accident and suffered brain injury with a devastating loss of intellectual functioning, started a state organization to help young adults with head injuries and their families. Other private ways of recovery might be immersion in nature, art, or religious meditation. Loving, working, and positive contemplation of beauty can lead grieving parents back to wholeness.

Chronic Problems Are Different

As horrible as deaths and some accidents and other acute emergencies can be, they have the advantage of closure, of finality. But as in the case of head injuries, parents can also face problems in the aftermath of a crisis that do not go away. Other chronic problems have more mysterious origins and cannot be pinned to one cause. For whatever reasons, some chronic problems ensure that the normal course of a child's growth from dependency to independent functioning in a competent adulthood becomes badly distorted.

Parents who have had autistic or retarded children early on face the fact that their children will be dependent for life. While still in infancy retarded children begin to show basic developmental deficits. Clearly, severely handicapped children are never going to grow up to be like most other people. In order to function well their parents have to find specialized environments and to start planning for the time when they can no longer be their children's caretakers or financial support.

When heretofore normal young adult children begin to have problems with functioning, or do not recover from an accident, parents are not prepared. The development of chronic mental illness in young adulthood is perhaps the worst-case scenario of an unforeseen catastrophe. Schizophrenia or depression may have a sudden onset or gradually emerge. Schizophrenia is particularly difficult to cope with. In the slide toward deterioration of functioning the young adult's whole self and personality may become cruelly distorted. Reality recedes, thinking is chaotic, and feelings are blunted as social interaction is severely impaired.

Parents despair because they can hardly recognize the ill person as the child they once knew. Pain lies in the memory of how much promise existed in the child and young adult before he or she became ill. As one despairing mother said of her schizophrenic daughter, "The daughter I raised is gone, or almost gone." Another parent voiced this same thought about a son: "You must say to yourself that the child you knew has died, and you must adopt the stranger who has taken his place."

Part of the agony of the road to mental illness is the difficulty of getting a certain, trustworthy diagnosis. Persons with problems in living do not always fit into neat categories and parents may not know what is really wrong for quite a while. Before getting to a full-blown diagnosis and recognition of a mental illness, there are usually long sagas of confusion and painful attempts to straighten out a young adult, who keeps landing in trouble or back on the family doorstep. The question keeps arising, "Is the problem one of a neurosis and mental illness or is this deviant behavior a form of immature malingering or selfish manipulation?" Since drug use is often involved, the picture becomes even more confused as to what is causing what. Parents become distraught trying to figure out the right thing to do.

If a child does become psychotic and is hospitalized there is a chance for recovery, but there is also a chance that there will be relapses and continuing fragility of personality for life. Parents with chronically mentally ill or impaired children begin a long career in frustration. The challenge is to cope and care for this impaired person, who when their illness flares up is incredibly difficult to deal with. At this point there are few outright cures, there are only available the palliative effects of medication and specially structured environments. Perhaps new successful treatments will be discovered in the future.

Parents can find it a nightmare to cope with debilitating mental illnesses because there is so little social or institutional help available for their children. If one lives in a state where you have to be dangerous to self or others in order to obtain involuntary hospitalization, and a young adult is not dangerous, there is little that parents can do with a sick person who does not think that he or she is sick and refuses treatment.

Private mental hospitals with excellent treatment programs may charge up to $950 a day. Medicaid or other insurance coverage is usually inadequate. Families must confront the fact that they cannot give or get what their mentally ill adult child needs, unless they are very, very rich. Even the wealthiest parent cannot ensure that a mentally ill son or daughter can become well; but they can pay for good care and make arrangements for their child's care after they themselves die. Most parents struggle on, doing the best they can, and the siblings know that when the parents die they will inherit the worry.

Other adult children never become psychotic or completely lose touch with reality, but they do become chronically emotionally impaired. Mild depressions, anxiety, panic attacks, eating disorders, and phobic symptoms can cause a great deal of suffering and keep a young adult from functioning at full capacity. The severity of these symptoms can range from near-disabling to mildly discomforting. The less serious forms of emotional problems can present difficult problems of diagnosis and puzzlements to parents over what is the best treatment. Where does ordinary unhappiness end and neurotic unhappiness begin? Who can tell from the outside the degree of mental pain or anxious fear that another person suffers? And who can tell whether the young person can learn to deal with these problems by going to work and exerting efforts at disciplined self-management?

If after therapy, emotional problems do not go away, it may be that the only alternative life offers is to bear up and function as best one can. Sometimes learning to live with a particularly difficult temperament is all that can be done. There is also the hope that anxiety or other mental suffering may diminish with age. Economic necessity and being forced to manage can sometimes push a slowly maturing person with a difficult emotional life into coping, otherwise known as getting themselves together. Parents should not give up too quickly in their demands for mature behavior and competent self-sufficiency, even when there is some chronic mental health problem.

But perhaps after many years have gone by, it becomes clear that no amount of time, encouragement, therapy, or economic necessity is going to make a difference in getting some adult child "straightened out." No matter how many attempts have been made for treatment or training it can appear that the young adult is incapacitated, however subtly, for normal independent life. Of course in this highly demanding society, a person does not have to be severely psychotic or severely mentally retarded to be a misfit.

Parents may finally have to face the fact that this adult child is not going to achieve what other people consider normal standards of economic and social success. How can parents deal with chronic maladaptation? It may help at this point to remember the truth, once succinctly stated in a televised drama, "All families have some members who can't make it." A long-term view of family history can make this clear. Once I knew a father, an outstanding achiever, indeed from a long line of Yankee achievers, who had a socially incompetent, eccentric son. This stoic father dealt with his disappointment by ruefully recalling that for centuries, "Every other generation of my family has produced its drop-outs." Fortunately, the go-getters over the years had accumulated enough land and wealth so there was a self-sustaining family farm to which his son could retreat. In the past, the extended family household often provided shelter for deviant, eccentric family members. When we read Truman Capote's story of his elderly fey cousin who flew kites with him and baked Christmas fruitcakes, we recognize a fragile person surviving on the fringes of an extended family household of kin.

For today's parents without a tradition of the extended family, the problem is far more difficult. If they can readopt an extended intergenerational model of the household, then a dependent adult child can live at home and work at some simple job. If parents think separate cooperating households are preferable for all family members, they can try to help their child find some cooperative living situation in which he or she can function. A child's permanent fragility and incompetence will necessitate some form of normalization, or the best life and work that can be achieved under the circumstances.

Parents in these situations face the problem of providing only help that does not further disable an adult child, or make him or her more dependent. The ideal goal is to find a solution that can be maintained after a parent has died.

If the child is suffering an addiction along with his or her other problems, the parents can rightly demand that this destructive habit be treated before any other help is offered. Addiction is one thing, permanent emotional and mental problems are another. But after long-term addictions are overcome some persons may be as ravaged as if they had suffered slight brain injury or had been wasted by a long-term physical disease. A person who has fought back to health from addiction may be without economic resources.

If there is no current drug use involved parents may decide to help as much as they are able — as long as they don't do anything for their child that he or she can do on his or her own. An adult who can work, should work. Adults who can care for themselves should do so. If they can, adults should pay or at least contribute to their own rehabilitative treatment, as a sign of maturity and because they work harder to recover when it's their own money.

Again, with cases of chronic impairment, we find downward economic movements in families. As already noted, even in the best of cases, many parents recognize that their children cannot do as well as *they* did because of the general downward pull of large socioeconomic forces. When recessions and depressions hit, normal well-functioning adult children of the upper middle class may be lucky to make it to the middle-middle class. If in addition an adult child is an emotionally fragile person, say one who has conquered a drug problem, or overcome severe neuroses, or psychosis, socioeconomic equilibrium will be even more elusive.

Careers and educations that have been derailed are not so easily reclaimed. When there are several adult children in a family, parents can end up having children in widely different economic strata. The emotionally stable stars go up, the troubled children go down. Siblings can consist of a corporate lawyer, a Ph.D. academic, and a struggling taxi driver. A daughter who marries well and has a successful career may live the American dream while her sister, recovering from schizophrenia, may hardly be able to manage a marginal life.

Parents adjusting to the different strengths, weaknesses, and life prospects that they may find in their children can struggle to reassert some equilibrium and keep the family together. Parents may mobilize to create, for the less fortunate members, opportunities they could never afford — opportunities such as family vacations, or presents of clothing, or family outings to cultural events. Siblings who are generous can help mitigate the disparity of social and economic outcomes in a family. Everyone needs to learn to share on behalf of family solidarity and compassion.

Once parents give up the illusion that certain problems can ever be solved, they can give up the exhausting mode befitting an emergency. Accepting a situation as permanent allows parents to mobilize their energy and resources in a different way. They can adopt the less frantic pace of the long-distance runner. The parental role can be redefined from one of launching independent achievers to one of loving and helping an adult with his or her difficult life course. Making the best of a sad reality is the challenge of tragedy. Tragedy can be defined as wasted potential; what might have been will never be.

Moral and Legal Tragedies

Mental and emotional problems may be less painful than the tragedies arising from immorality and crime in the family. When I taught in a women's prison, the pain and shame felt by the prisoners' parents added to the burdens the prisoners bore. Many of their parents were raising the grandchildren while their daughters were serving their sentences. A large number of these parents were immigrants who had made heroic efforts to come to America so that they and their children could have a better life. Their dreams had been shattered. Often these prisoners' troubles with the law had come from drug addictions that spawned prostitution and other crimes.

As a middle-class suburbanite, I could ponder similar experiences of parents I know whose children had been arrested and run afoul of the law. Often these infractions were minor and left behind on the young adult's road to maturity — but not always. Again, the trouble was usually drugs, for drug use is no respecter of class lines; it is an equal-opportunity destroyer. The other motivation for crime — greed for material things — also tempts middle-class persons into cutting corners and stealing — as with the young white-collar criminals one encounters.

The tragedy of criminal behavior and incarceration can happen in middle and upper-class families, although each of these families probably feels fairly isolated in their ordeal. Occasionally, as with Jimmy Carter's jailed nephew, the plight of the black sheep of a prominent family comes to light. Other cases of criminal middle-class youth, such as New York's preppie murderer and the felonies of children of celebrities are widely publicized.

In my experience, crises of crime in the middle-class family seem to be of two different kinds. There is the one-time crime that seems related to some particular condition — an addiction, or a temporary temptation for a vulnerable person in a time of stress. Then there is the antisocial adult child who has always been a problem from the beginning, or at least from adolescence on. The rebellious young adult, usually a male, never grows out of an adolescent stage of fighting against all authorities. A negative identity becomes established; transgression after transgression solidifies the child's reputation as a deviant bad apple or near-psychopath. Penalties mount with repeated infractions and the repeated failures of rehabilitation efforts; the course is a downhill one and prison is the final result.

Parents suffer three times over when their adult children act wrongfully and get punished: once for the personal shame and disappointment over their child's moral failure, and then again out of empathy when their child is in pain, however much it is deserved. Finally a parent can despair over the harm their child has caused to others — the victims, other family members, those other mentors who have trusted and invested in the young adult. Usually a parent can never rectify these wrongs in any way. One may pay back money that has been stolen, but one cannot undo other kinds of harm.

A parent bitterly bemoans the fact that the basic expectation of raising an honorable upright person has been dashed. Life is full enough of dreadful things and sorrows that cannot be helped, so why did this child have to do such a destructive thing and create so much pain for everyone concerned? Despite their justifiable disappointment, most parents still want to do the right thing for their erring child. No matter what, my child is my child, and if a young adult accepts responsibility and is repentant, then most parents will do everything they can to forgive and provide necessary support. Parents procure legal advice, and often pay for it; they support their children through the ordeal of trial, and if necessary visit them in prison. In the middle classes as well as in immigrant groups, parents help raise their grandchildren while young parents are incarcerated.

If, however, an adult child commits a crime and remains defiant and hostile, unwilling to change or seek rehabilitation, parents may have to back off to let natural consequences play their harsh role in breaking through denial. If you cannot believe in the innocence of a person, you cannot. Mrs. Oswald, and other less than satisfactory parental models, may have always been sure that their sons were innocent, but every parent may not be so self-deceiving.

Every parent, however, wants a child to benefit from all the due processes of law that citizens are entitled to. But if a person is truly guilty it may be morally destructive for him or her to escape all punishment for his or her misdeed. The parental desire to believe the best and to keep a child from suffering is totally understandable, but a commitment to justice cannot be so selective that one's children are not to be held morally accountable. The practice of exempting our loved ones from the legal and moral system, if generalized, would destroy our society. It seems wrong to try and totally foil the legal system on behalf of one's child.

I would not agree with the action of the father in Andre Dubus's short story who hides the evidence of his daughter's hit-and-run killing of a young man walking on a dark country road. The father and daughter lie and collude in a cover-up so no one will find out; neither the police nor the young man's family ever know what happened. Dubus has this father, a devout religious believer, justify himself in his daily dialogues with God. The father asserts that if one of his sons had come to him for help in a similar situation, he would immediately have called the police and summoned an ambulance. But as the father of a young woman, he could not bear to watch his daughter suffer. He admits to God that in the case of his only daughter, "I love her more than I love truth."

This is a moving story of a father's love. But what is left undiscussed are the possible consequences of the father's helping his daughter lie and deceive others to avoid taking responsibility for her actions. In effect, this father by his example and his actions has weakened her adherence to truth and reality; he has also left her with a bad conscience for life. She can conclude as well that because she is a woman she cannot be expected to be as morally responsible as her brothers. A parent, no matter how painful it is, has an obligation to see justice done and the truth upheld, inside and outside the family. When it comes to either blame or excuses the idea has too often been defended that a different standard of morality should apply within the family. I think this is only true in the positive direction. We may owe our families more than justice — i.e., love's generosity — but we cannot let them get away with unjust behavior or let ourselves treat them with less than the duties due a stranger. If you cannot hit a stranger without assault charges, why should a husband be able to hit his wife?

Intimacy and loving commitment does not excuse a parent countenancing immoral behavior in the family. I think a parent can understand that if he or she gives in to pressure or morally doubtful pleas or manipulations, then an adult child will be encouraged to replicate such behavior with others. It is no small thing to let others do wrong; it damages their character. Anyone we respect we wish to hold to the same standards as everyone else we respect.

In certain cases, however, some uncertainty arises as to what moral standards should apply. There is the possibility that an adult child is mentally incompetent or mentally impaired when engaged in wrongdoing. Parents can conclude that their child was deranged and not responsible for his immoral or criminal conduct. One sympathizes with parents whose adult child has done something bizarre and horrible, like the parents of the young deranged woman who shot children playing in a schoolyard.

A notorious public case that brought up the problem of mental illness and moral responsibility was John Hinckley's assassination attempt on President Reagan. The Hinckleys, as a successful, upstanding, well-to-do family, had to face the painful fact that their son had tried to kill the president and had grievously wounded Jim Brady — in order, he said, to impress Jodie Foster the movie actress.

The Hinckley case was an interesting example of how difficult it is to tell whether a young adult's maladaptive behavior is free and voluntary or an involuntary manifestation of mental illness. In the course of John Hinckley's unsatisfactory young adulthood, the Hinckley parents had tried various measures and treatments to help their drifting, incompetent son to attend school, to work, to live alone, and become independent of their support. They had finally turned him out of the house on the advice of a psychologist advocating "toughlove." After his bizarre crime they came to believe that his immature, eccentric, and violent behavior was the result of the disordered thought processes of schizophrenia, and not a free and willful defiance of moral standards.

If and when serious mental illness is causing symptomatic behavior it is morally important for our legal system to recognize the condition as an exception that proves the rule of normal responsibility. In hindsight, a case like Hinckley's cried out for hospitalization and treatment, rather than a strategy of cutting him off from his family's help. The Hinckleys faced a problem similar to other parents of troubled young adults: "Is my child manipulating us in order to avoid growing up, or is something mentally wrong?" In an ambiguous case, where there has been gradual mental deterioration over time, it is sometimes hard to tell what is going on until a final breakdown occurs.

Then again deviant behavior is not always easily classified as either illness or moral failure. There are many actions that at the same time are morally wrong, illegal, and yet seem to be partly the result of mental impairment or mental illness. The unfortunate parents who find out that their sons are pedophiles are in the no-man's-land of repugnant behaviors that are morally despicable, criminal, and in all probability, a form of neurotic compulsion. Drug addictions too may start out as free voluntary moral choices and at some point turn into involuntary, out-of-control behavior described as disease.

The problem for any bystander, and particularly a loving parent, is to discern when a loss of personal control has occurred. At that point involuntary treatment may be indicated, if it can be managed. Parents who believe involuntary treatment is necessary often face the disconcerting problem of turning their adult child over to some institution or authority in the face of his protests. Parents are tortured by the decision to call the police or to initiate involuntary commitment procedures. They can only hope that in the long run their child will thank them for their actions, or at least understand that they were necessary.

Perhaps one of the worst things faced by a parent is violence committed by one's adult child. To have an adult child who is abusing his spouse or child produces an acute conflict. Yet the impetus for action is also stronger when the harm that is being done affects other family members to whom one also has an obligation. A grandparent, for instance, has a responsibility to protect his or her grandchild if he or she is suffering abuse.

At the opposite extreme is the parental experience of having an adult child falsely accused of child abuse. False accusations and other conflicts enmeshing innocent sons or daughters with the law or social sanctions can create a great deal of parental suffering on behalf of their adult children. I have known a case of false accusation of child abuse against wonderful young parents who were totally dedicated to their children. These young parents and both sets of grandparents suffered terribly as the clumsy bureaucratic system ground on in its investigation. The dismissal of the case and eventual vindication left a family exhausted by the ordeal.

When it is the case that a child has been falsely accused or is suffering some social injustice, then the support and advocacy of parents and the rest of the family is crucial. Many young people, even in the United States, have been prisoners of conscience in the cause of peace or civil rights. Parents in many situations have badgered authorities, and have been instrumental in getting justice for their children.

Can Suffering Be Avoided? Will a Parent Only Be as Happy as Their Least Happy Child?

Inevitably, life includes suffering, and family life is no exception. The paradox of kinship is that while having children brings an increase of joy and happiness, bonding empathetically with your child opens a parent to vicarious suffering. When those we love suffer, then we suffer too. When misfortunes occur in the lives of our children, we become enmeshed in their struggles.

Can such suffering and struggle on behalf of others be avoided? No, not if we choose to be connected and attached with loving bonds. The Stoics sought to master suffering by rigid suppression and denial of all emotions and attachments. They cultivated personal detachment from all fear, desire and personal affection. The ideal state in stoic strategies is *apatheia,* or the absence of feeling. Once complete emotional detachment is reached, then a person need never fear harm to self or others. One looks unmoved upon all suffering, yours and that of those related to you.

To those whose primary goal in life is to love and be loved, stoic detachment is a completely inadequate, if not repugnant, solution to the problem of suffering. Nor can most of us take comfort in new-age ideologies proclaiming evil to an illusion that does not exist. Evil and tragedies do exist, and they occur in our lives and in the lives of those close to us. Some awful things cannot be denied or remedied; they simply have to be borne with as much fortitude as we can muster.

There is no foolproof way to explain away tragedy or to justify human suffering. The only thing that can be said for suffering is that sometimes it helps some people to be more empathetic with the pain of others; and that it makes us deeply appreciative of the good things in life. For some not completely understood reason, many persons who have suffered much, and been able to continue loving others, appear to be the same persons who are most full of joy and gratitude. Why? Is their heart or capacity for empathy enlarged or stretched by suffering? Or is it that people who risk more and become deeply connected to others leave themselves open to being hurt, but also have more resources for comfort?

Once you have entered upon the path of parenthood, you come to recognize that loving your children makes you vulnerable to pain in many different ways, but that love of other is also the surest source of joy.

It has been said that "parents can only be as happy as the least happy of their children." This is an often heard claim but I think it shows an incorrect understanding of how complex human beings can be. Human consciousness is so complex that multiple themes can play themselves out in an endless variety of interweaving patterns over time. A parent can truthfully say that he or she shares a child's current suffering, or will always grieve over a child's death, or a child's moral failure, and yet at the same time be able to experience happiness and joy.

Unhappiness and pain can exist, either directly or from vicarious suffering, and be ready to surface into a parent's consciousness, but so can many other more positive memories. Moments of happiness can occur even in the midst of the most acute stages of grieving. People report that in the midst of tears at a funeral, the beauty of music or a shaft of sunlight can be a source of joy. Gratitude for the kindnesses of friends and family can surge up within the most desperate sufferer in many torturous situations. Wakes alternate regularly between sadness and merriment.

If this is so, then suffering and rejoicing with others, mutually shared sorrow and delight, can be interwoven in a person's inner life. Mature individuals have also learned to actively direct their focus of attention away from the self and to other things and to other people and tasks in the world. We can move away from pain to take up our work, and even move to savor positive pleasures and satisfactions. While I would not agree with all his writings, when Marcus Aurelius says that "happiness is an inward power of the soul," he speaks the truth. The human spirit is incredibly resilient. While the tapestry of the heart can have black threads and blood red stitches worked into the pattern, its overall design can blazon happiness.

CHAPTER EIGHT

Getting Ready for the Final Act of Parenthood, or How to Manage Old Age and Dying Better Than King Lear

In middle and late middle age you are still healthy and your children are grown up. *Now* is the time to prepare yourself and your children for your old age and death. Already your oversolicitous adult children may have begun telling you what to do and how to live. As one aging New Yorker complained, "I wish my daughter would stop trying to get me to go and live near her in God-forsaken Columbus, Ohio; can you imagine me in the Midwest?" No, I could not. But I could envision her, like King Lear and other aging parents, forced to live in ways she could not abide. An old person does not have to be as rash, arrogant, and unfair as Lear, or have spawned a Goneril or Regan, to end one's life badly.

If you want a good old age, a good death, and good order in your family affairs after you die, you must make an effort while you still have all your wits about you, while you are in firm control of your money and social clout. Nothing can ever be counted on to happen simply by itself. Your adult children must be enlisted in your plans for your future. In late middle age parents have to confront their old age and dying, clarify their family goals, and prepare for their demise by arranging practical details. Why should you condemn your children to reading books on how to manage their aging parents? If anyone in the family is going to consult a gerontologist about the difficulties of your aging, let it be you, beforetime.

Overcoming Denial
and Facing Up to Death and Decline

Sometime in your fifties the fact begins to sink in that you, too, are going to get old and die. You may not feel any different inside but the mirror keeps reflecting an aging face and figure. Your children may be beginning to show their own signs of aging with their gray hair or male balding patterns. One aging mother said that she had coped with the loss of her looks by transferring her narcissistic vanity to her beautiful youthful children. When *they* began to suffer the depredations of age, it was a blow. Mortality and the fleetingness of time became real.

Our parents and older relatives die, then friends and contemporaries start dying of heart attacks, breast cancers, brain tumors, and other lethal maladies. People who were the powerful movers and shakers of one's youth appear old and frail. So many of yesterday's heroes, politicians, movie stars, and celebrities have died, that we begin to have trouble remembering who is alive and who is dead. The obituaries page becomes fascinating as we know more and more of the featured population.

Reading obituaries I often give in to bouts of magic thinking and try to figure out what these benighted people did wrong. Are they dying because they continued to smoke, drink, eat poorly, refuse exercise, or indulge in unsafe sex? I of course, would never do such dangerous things and I feel momentarily safe. Besides, as my husband says, we are not dead yet, why should we give in to mere probabilities and conclude that we too will succumb? But, alas, eventually the reality principle forces us to accede to the fact that we cannot live forever by taking good care of ourselves and thinking positive thoughts. And how will we be written up in our own death notices? At least as parents of adult children we can be assured that our obituaries will not end with that chilling line: "there are no known survivors."

Once death is accepted, our thoughts turn to our survivors. One last parental challenge becomes clear: I must age and die well. How can I model an exemplary exit, an honorable and commendable last act? My children will be watching.

In the nature of the life cycle, humans have to learn how to be old and die from those who go before them. Traditionally, one's older kin should be mentors and the culture should give some guidance in the art of dying. But today, relatives are scattered, we do not regularly attend deathbeds, and our culture is faltering. As adults in their prime, our children have their own aging and death before them. Can I as their aging parent muster my resources and give them a usable scenario for their own old age?

A technologically sophisticated medicine is producing new turbulent seas at the end of our voyage that must be navigated without reliable charts. While we are grateful to have access to medical marvels, we also have new problems that have not been faced before. The miracles of modern medicine can give us longer but not always healthier lives at the end. Our physicians cannot guarantee that we will be spry and self-sufficient forever, only the blessed few luck out and drop dead at an advanced age while still pretty much in possession of the mental and physical powers of their prime. Their adult children receive a telephone call informing them of their parents' "sudden" death.

More of the population suffer diminishment and fragility in old-old age; not many ninety-year-olds are healthy enough to fend for themselves, or rich enough to hire an army of attendants to care for them day and night in their own homes. Late middle age therefore is the time to get organized and enlist your children in your preferred strategies for the next stages of life. Although "ripeness is all," ripeness can hardly last forever. The family that in midcycle is made up of equally competent adults will shift in the balance of power as parents age. This shift makes it imperative that parents think about their goals and make plans that will carry out their values. Whatever one's decisions about old age and death, it will all go better if you persuade your adult children to cooperate fully and help you. Of course, some grown children defensively resist the fact that their parents are aging. They have to be forced to recognize that no one is immortal. Everyone will become old, one way or another.

What Is an Ideal Old Age?

Is there one ideal for old age in American culture? Not really. There seem to be a plurality of preferred goals, although every older person would like to have enough money, resources, and health to be free to choose their ideal life-style There are Florida sunbathers who want to play every day, and other old people who intend to die with their boots on still in harness. In between the extremes, there are other patterns of elderly retirement and part-time avocations.

I subscribe to the view that old age makes us more individuated, unique, and idiosyncratic. One's adult children have to realize this and give up any general blueprint they may harbor about what is good for the elderly. Unless severely brain damaged, we tend to become more completely the selves we have been fashioning over the years. (Unfortunately, this means that selfish, mean, irritable parents can become far worse to live with!)

Some aging individuals raised in a tradition of extended multi-generational families will want to live with their adult children when they are old. They simply assume that old people live with their grown children who take care of them. In the past both economic necessity and a cultural ideal of family made joint residence the obvious solution for aging parents who need assistance as they become more fragile. Even without economic pressures an extended household can be an ideal solution for some families.

An elderly Alabama aunt of mine lived happily with her eldest daughter's family after she became a widow. "I hated living alone," she said. This aunt had come from a Southern tradition of extended households and all her life she had been a homemaker and hostess — gregarious, intelligent, delightfully charming, and beloved by all. She was very domestic, did needlework, and loved helping her career daughter and son-in-law with the cooking and other household tasks. She adored her grandchildren and was adored by them. She was also the soul of tact and made sure that her daughter and son-in-law had their privacy, although they would share many social events such as going to church and family functions.

In this outgoing and close family, filial piety within a Christian belief system remained a strong value shared by all. I remember my aunt saying that as she lost consciousness from a small stroke she had not felt fear but had thought, "Now I am going to join my ancestors." Death was not terrible for her, but losing her mind and memory would have been a horrible fate. My aunt had even given up bridge in her seventies because she could not bear perchance to play less than brilliantly.

Other typical curtailments of activities due to age were also necessary as her arthritic pain increased. But since Southern ladies do not complain, or fail in politesse or cheerfulness, she did not ever become bitter — about anything. "I have no room for hate in my heart," she said in talking over past wrongs she had suffered from her mean-spirited stepmother. She enjoyed each remaining day she was given, wrote letters, crocheted, and began to reread Shakespeare as an intellectual project in her last year.

Why not hold up this traditional family pattern of joint residence as the best possible solution for old age? After all, a parent who has borne, reared, and given emotional and financial support to a child, should be able to expect aid in return at the end of life. If there is an affectionate bond between parent and child there is also deep gratitude. Our general cultural prescription for being a good adult person includes filial piety, or the duty to care for one's old parents. The obligation to honor your mother and father is commanded generally, even when there are not intense emotional affinities in the family. It also says in the Bible, "Be not impatient with your old father even though his mind should fail."

Family bonds and loyalty are important for any society and for any ideal of virtuous character we can imagine. Many parents who have cared dutifully for their own elderly parents have provided models for their grown children. When parents become old, I think it can be right and good for the elderly to live with their children.

If aging parents and their children choose this path, then practical provisions can be made for this eventuality early on. My cousin had initially built her house with a private wing for the day when her mother would come to live with her. Many people who build or remodel homes create an in-law apartment for their aging parents to live with them. Aging parents, for their part, may arrange their homes for joint residence, or buy a residence with their old age in mind.

Help and loving attention from one's adult children will always be expected in old age, but many, many parents do not wish to be the slightest bit dependent upon their children. They definitely do not want to live with them if they can help it. Many aging persons in the population wish to maintain their privacy and do not favor the multigenerational extended household as their cultural ideal. How many times have we heard people say that they do not want to be a burden on their children — and "being a burden" is interpreted as living with the adult child's family.

Parents can prefer not to live with their adult children for other reasons as well. Some families don't get along well enough to live together. The parents and children do not share values or the same tastes, and living together under any circumstances would be difficult for everyone. Incompatible adult children are not likely to be eagerly pushing their parents to come and join their households. Other aging folks, like myself, would rather not reside with adult children or anyone else. I am rather contemplative by nature and like solitude. I am not domestic in my interests and do not miss hustle and bustle. If I can read, I don't need constant company.

Other parents are totally committed to self-sufficiency and autonomy, on strict principle, no matter what. They would literally rather die than go to a hospital or ever get into a dependent relationship with either their children or a caretaking institution. Many older adults fear that they will end up being warehoused and abused in some dreadful nursing home. How many times have we heard people say that they never, never, want to go to a nursing home. If an older person considers such a prospect a fate worse than death, he or she will go to drastic lengths to avoid it. I know of one strong-minded woman of seventy who refused to go to a hospital for anything. She was determined to die at home by the simple expedient of standing on her rights and refusing to leave her house. She was quite willing to forego the extra years of life that high tech medical care might give her, in exchange for the surety that she would never end up chronically ill in a hospital or nursing home. (It is interesting in the obituaries to see how few people die at home.)

Is the demand never to go to an institution reasonable? I don't think so. Suppose the strong-minded elderly woman had needed an appendectomy? This would be a minor operation that is routinely successful and does not require long recuperation or nursing care. But in addition to brief stays in the hospital, going into an institution like a nursing home may become necessary. While adult children usually resist giving up the care of their old parents, elderly ill individuals may have nursing needs at the end of life that are in excess of their families' caretaking capacities. As always, a lot will depend upon the financial and economic circumstances of the individual person and the current state of law, health-care institutions, and insurance plans available when and in which locale one becomes old and ill. The economic and social resources of one's adult children will also be a factor.

One solution for those who do not ever wish to live with their children is to have saved up plenty of money. If you have enough income you can stay home and pay compatible people to come in and take care of you. This arrangement leaves you in your own home and still in charge. I have watched several well-to-do people create mininursing homes in their apartments, with constant nursing companions and frequent visits from their physicians. From time to time, these affluent elderly persons may go to the hospital for brief emergency care, but they are generally assured that their money will enable them to hire nurses, and come home to die in their own beds.

When an old person gets to stay in his or her usual surroundings, personal social habits of visiting and neighborly networks can be more easily maintained. If an adult child lives nearby and can oversee the household, there is enough backup support and filial attention, even if every bit of care is not given by the daughter or son. Certainly in raising children we do not think it wrong when children are cared for by capable persons other than their parents. I think a family should apply the same caretaking standards to the old that work well with small children: We aim for as much autonomy, independence, and self-direction as possible.

One of my admired role models was a spirited but fragile eighty-six-year-old woman who used to say: "Please don't do that for me; my rule is to do everything I still can without help." Happily, she was well off, so she could afford to have admirable helper companions who made it possible for her to maintain her own apartment and her own lively social intellectual life, apart from her attentive son. Her son who lived nearby visited and called frequently; he insisted on full-time round-the-clock-care, which she accepted, although she hated to deplete the family estate. Her aging was an ideal, semi-independent style of life.

But sometimes, even with affluence, there is no nearby adult child to oversee a household. Families are small and may be dispersed. Grown children cannot come home again, and this is especially true of the most successful progeny who are ensconced in demanding careers. It can be too disruptive to have an old parent change locales. While reading obituaries I also note where the surviving adult children reside in relation to the deceased. Today most women will be working and hard-pressed for family time. The harassed middle classes in hard economic times can find that they have little time and limited money. The middle generation in a three-tiered family can be overstressed and more or less crunched if they are trying to care for their old parents and their adolescent children.

The increasing habit of delaying marriage and childbearing may mean that it will be more likely in the future that a parent's old age and death will take place while their adult children are rearing young children — a period when resources of energy, time, and money are notably depleted. Those of us now preparing for old age can easily imagine our own children as middle-aged persons with a lot fewer resources than we have. The expectations garnered from older traditional family patterns, when most people did not move so much or live so long, will have to be adjusted.

When an elderly parent begins to need more help in daily routines, there will be a real dilemma when the family is scattered. Often a grown child, usually a daughter, of course, tries by long-distance calls and frequent trips to arrange and supervise care. Long-distance caretaking often becomes unsatisfactory. Another good solution for those who are fairly well-to-do is to enter a well-run retirement institution. With the increasing proportion of old people in the population, creative retirement communities have been developed that can meet the needs of today's changing family patterns, as well as those who have alienated families, or no families.

These communities often have several stages of care available. There are apartments or townhouses for completely independent living, hotel-like facilities for those who can no longer cook or care for themselves, and hospital wings for those requiring constant nursing care. An old person or one member of a couple can move back and forth between these levels of assisted care, although the direction is usually toward the hospital. Once settled in such a retirement community a parent and their adult children can be assured that the individual will have as much independence as possible, along with the comfort of knowing that nursing care will be available when it is needed.

The best of these institutions, often subsidized by religious denominations, are full of amenities, community social life, and intellectual stimulation. Life in these ideal settings with compatible people can be somewhat like going on an extended cruise or like attending an elder hostel. (The fact that death is the final destination is unavoidable.) These institutions encourage celebrations, friendships, family contacts, religious practice, and keeping up with the world. These communities also provide security and mutual aid between age mates. The fact that everyone in the residence is old is offset by the fact that people like and understand their own generation. Those who are well volunteer their time taking care of those in the hospital wings. Since one joins voluntarily by buying into the community while still healthy, it is a form of institutionalization that is without the horrors faced by the poor in poorly run nursing homes.

If an aging person or couple chooses this solution, then their task is to do research and start investigating residences before any emergency arises. It may take time to find a compatible community that is financially sound. In different areas there may be other informal group living arrangements that can be looked into as well. Many older people are reproducing the traditional patterns of siblings sharing a household, but the siblings are "fictive kin" chosen for compatibility. In any event, adult children should be consulted and sold on any proposed venture. When they will be coming to visit often, they can also serve as outside observers to the quality of care extended as well as monitors of their parent's well-being.

Adult children and family support will be even more important if an aging person has to go into a less well-appointed nursing home. When this less-than-ideal solution becomes necessary, adult children have to serve as advocates and intercessors for their parents. They should be ready to give supplementary care and attention, and to be sure that their parents are not suffering from lack of stimulation and companionship. I remember meeting a birdlike ninety-five-year-old woman in a poorly run nursing home who had been a milliner. She was now reduced to making miniature hats out of tinfoil. As an immigrant from Poland, she had never married, and outlived all her relatives. She had no visitors and was the last leaf on the family tree. This was a sad situation but it is far worse when elderly people who end up in poor nursing homes *have* adult children but are abandoned by them. They then can echo King Lear's cry, "How sharper than a serpent's tooth it is to have a thankless child!" These parents suffer from loneliness but even more painfully from their disappointment that they have raised a child who could be callous and selfish enough to neglect an aged parent.

Middle-aged parents who have good relationships with attentive children should begin, with their children's help, to devise an acceptable strategy for their old age. Casting a cold eye on aging, parents should shake off romantic hopes and plan for the worst possible consequences as well as the best. Different stages of physical decline, even dementia, God forbid, should be taken into account in a contingency strategy. Once everyone in the family has a clear map, then one's doctor, lawyer, and friends should also be drawn into the plan. Taking thought beforehand can help make one's aging and decline proceed with fewer uncertainties, anxieties, backstage plots, and family conflicts over who will do what, and when.

In the end, finding suitable arrangements and caretakers may be easier than coping with the spiritual and psychological challenges of the inevitable diminishments and growing incapacities of aging. Robert Browning seemed self-deceived when he burbled, "Grow old along with me! The best is yet to be." I see old age as an arduous physical, mental, and emotional struggle against unfavorable odds. Aging seems a completely uncongenial enterprise no matter how much life wisdom we may acquire. Admittedly, there is great stress at the beginning of adult life when one labors to bear and rear children, but these are positive, hopeful, upward-and-onward-into-the-future projects. Going ever more quickly toward death is different — downhill all the way, as Leonard Woolf described his last years.

Clearly fortitude and character are going to be needed to get through old age morally and psychologically unscathed. Can I manage not to be self-absorbed, narcissistic, inflexible, and self-indulgent? Those who triumph over old age seem interested in everything, surprised by nothing, as they listen to all. Their adult children and their friends are not bored by their conversation. The victorious keep learning, loving, meditating, and appreciating beauty — and they don't whine and litter the environment with criticism and sour complaints. Many old persons inspire admiration when they maintain their strength of character in the face of pain, discomfort, and disability. I try to prepare for the inevitable losses of old age by musing on the war cry of ancient Anglo-Saxon warriors doomed to die in their last battle against overwhelming odds: "Courage has got to be harder, heart the stouter, spirit the sterner, as our strength weakens."

Strength weakens. Only a stout heart can manage the gallant final engagement that edifies the survivors. "Now we will show the world how to die," said Pope John XXIII, as he entered his last illness. The art of dying has not totally been discounted in our culture.

The Art of Dying

In the seventeenth century there were many treatises on the art of dying. We might not be attracted to some of the stratagems recommended — such as sleeping in your coffin or keeping a skull on your desk. But the basic message of these books still applies: To die well you must live well each day, to prepare for the day and the moment when your soul is required of you. If you have unfinished business with your children or any reconciliations to effect with anyone, hurry up and do it. You may be able to have an extended farewell with your family, or you may not.

This generation cannot count on dying swiftly. We have the dilemmas of the intensive care unit to worry about. Medicine may be able to save my life, but leave me in some dreadful condition, hovering between death and life, dependent upon life-support machines. Many a middle-aged parent, like myself, can be less frightened of death and more frightened of permanently losing self-consciousness without dying. The idea of living on and on like a zombie in a persistent coma seems dreadful. Contemplating the pitiable condition of many old and demented persons barely kept alive by machines induces the middle-aged to take steps to avoid the clutches of excessive medical technology. Adult children should be enlisted as allies in this campaign.

When some medical intervention can sustain bodily life but cannot cure or restore psychological functioning, many of us will assert our right as a patient to refuse treatment. We can educate ourselves about living wills, health-care proxies, advanced directives about future treatment decisions, and durable powers of attorney. We recognize the need to prepare for death, and then talk to our doctors, our spouses, and our adult children, to be sure that they understand our wishes. I know it is impossible to cover all contingencies beforehand, but we can articulate our general approach to dying and our desire for a good death.

A good death for most people is a death that is neither premature, nor prolonged, and a death with a minimum of mental or physical suffering. There should be as little loss of personhood or human dignity as possible. Despite some general fears, most people die peacefully, and we sometimes see ideal deaths. I think here of my eighty-eight-year-old grandmother, who died suddenly in her sleep at home in bed after a full day of social and business transactions devoted to her calves, farms, and baby chicks. Her rural life was full of hard work, much deprivation, and many trials, but her death was as good a death as you can have. The only better death I have ever heard of was that of the theologian Teilhard de Chardin who was instantly struck down by a stroke after saying Easter Sunday mass, while drinking champagne with friends.

Deaths come with all varieties and degrees of suffering. We are made most anxious by the fate of those persons who die isolated in hospitals painfully trussed up with tubes and machines. The final illness may be the third or fourth illness or crisis staved off by the intervention of medical technology. Pain and suffering accompany each of the illnesses in which death is averted, and recovery is hardly ever complete. Few persons survive these prolonged bouts of suffering without diminishments of their rational acuity or personality — losses which, if recognized, cause them even more suffering.

There has to be a better way to go. While inventing technology is an innately human activity, and medical technology is a great gift to humanity, we have to learn to control runaway technology or it will control us. The technological imperative must be resisted so that instead of deciding to do anything and everything that *can* be done, we will only do what should be done, all things considered. No one wants to be denied medical treatment that will do some good and restore a person to healthy functioning, but futile burdensome treatment that only prolongs dying should be refused and avoided.

If refusals and patient's rights are going to be honored, one's adult children must be informed and ready to be one's advocate. I think it is a responsibility of middle-aged parents to reflect upon the different eventualities of the dying process and then instruct their adult children as to their decisions. Otherwise adult children may be too emotionally distraught to make agonizing decisions with wisdom. The more detail given to them for guidance, the better.

In my own case I am sure that I do not want to be aggressively treated and have my body kept alive on machines when there is no hope for restoration of self-conscious functioning. Medically futile treatment seems an assault on human dignity and a waste of valuable resources. And if I am in a permanently unconscious state I do not want to be fed food and water through tubes to keep my body alive. Indeed if I am completely demented and am no longer in any way able to interact with others, and I get pneumonia (the old person's friend), let me die peacefully without antibiotics pulling me back into a more prolonged dying.

Of course it is also clear that pain can deform human living when it is intense and prolonged. If I am certainly dying, I do not want my doctor to be stingy with pain medication. If the pain medication to keep me comfortable also shortens my life, that is fine with me. Like Freud and other stalwart souls, I would like to be as conscious as possible for as long as possible, even at the price of some pain; but when it gets too bad then getting enough pain medication is important. There seems to be a scandalous lack of medical sophistication about pain control, and I want to go to a doctor and hospital that understands that pain can be controlled and should be controlled. I want my children to fight for me in this matter.

The hospice approach of gin and heroin cocktails in humane surroundings seems the right way to die. I will look for a hospice program in my neighborhood in case I need it. It seems scandalous that at this point in our odd health system medicare will pay for acute, high technological care but not for home hospice nurses. If you have money you can pay for hospice care at home.

We should fight off death as long as we can, but when it is hopeless we can bow to the inevitable and attempt to make a peaceful exit. But accepting death is different from affirming it. I can never see death as anything but a monstrous affront to self-consciousness and the desire to experience life. How horrible it seems to be forced to break off the connections and bonds with society and our world. Whatever our ultimate spiritual destiny, and I am a believer in eternal life, there is deep sorrow in separating from the precious earth and the children we love.

Despite my hatred of dying, I aspire to resign myself to it with some serenity of spirit. I may rage against the dying of the light philosophically, but I hope that in practice I will be able to accept my common mortality with good grace. To this end, I want to be able to talk to my children about dying while I'm still alive. In my childhood death was a completely tabu subject, inducing anxiety in conversations and even in private thoughts. You were considered ill-mannered or morbid if you dwelt on this, the most obvious and certain fact of human existence. An effort was made to make death invisible and unmentionable. Persons with any property were enjoined to make wills and families bought burial plots and went to funerals, but that was about it for death and dying.

Then in certain academic circles death and dying came out of the closet. Books, college courses, magazine articles, and documentaries poured forth, increasing an awareness of death. The modern American way of death was exposed as full of euphemisms, evasions, and needless expense. Efforts were made to recover the art of dying and support for the dying. Families were helped to understand and help their members die in a humane way according to their beliefs and values.

In pluralistic America parents may hold to one meaning of death and their children to another. Death may be seen as the final end of the individual — except what lives on in the memories of others. Or death may be viewed as the beginning of a new life with God in a new form. Death, for those influenced by

Eastern approaches to religious truth, may be the rejoining of the world soul, or the reentry into cycles of reincarnation and rebirth. Different philosophies and religious views of death are accompanied by beliefs about dying and the appropriate rites, or lack of rites that should be performed by the family survivors. Hamlet and Antigone may have disagreed about what duties they owed the dead, but like most of humanity they did recognize the fact of family obligations to the departed.

Aging parents should make choices about which of their inherited beliefs or which of the available cultural beliefs they accept or reject and leave instructions for their children. Some individuals will want their children to be sure that appropriate last rites are carried out. They should leave detailed directions about the disposal of their bodies or organs, and what kind of burial or cremation they wish. Many will want to plan their funerals. I, for instance, do not want any eulogizing remarks or any hymns with sexist or militaristic language — no onward Christian soldiers for me. Others simply may not care, since after death it will be irrelevant. Let my children bury me any way that they want, or skip it entirely.

But it does seem to be a last parental duty to buy burial plots, if needed, and leave a will so that disorder will not reign after one's death. By making a will, parents can dispose of their property and expedite settling their affairs. Parents in earlier times took making a will very seriously — either because they faced death so much more openly or were more concerned with property and family relations. Sometimes they tried to make appropriate provisions for the different life prospects of their different children. A will was an important last statement from beyond the grave.

Disliked in-laws sometimes came off with short shrift. A widow in Shakespeare's time said, "Yet so I do intend the same as that my said son-in-law Mr. Herbert Finch shall never have possession of the same goods. ... " Shakespeare's will also revealed, by its special provisions excluding one son-in-law, his worries that a daughter's husband was unreliable. This adult daughter and her husband had immediately before Shakespeare's last illness been publicly excommunicated in Shakespeare's local parish. When

Lear moans of "the infamy that it is to be a parent," the cry may have reflected Shakespeare's bitter experiences of parenthood.

Today Americans more often seem to divide their property up completely equally in order to avoid squabbles over favoritism. Of course, when money is involved it is not always possible to avoid conflict. Some struggles over whether elderly parents should remarry are in reality fights over who will inherit how much of the parent's money. Selfish human nature and sibling rivalries are always realities in life. At least by trying to be fair and leaving a detailed will, parents try to leave a legacy of peace. They have tried to exercise prudent control. But can there be too much control in modern dying? What of recent movements for suicide, assisted suicide, and euthanasia as ways for aging parents to bring about death?

Suicide, Assisted Suicide, and Euthanasia

I do not think that suicide, assisted suicide, or euthanasia are appropriate means to control death and dying. While aging parents should try to plan for their decline and prudently prepare for death, these particular strategies are morally counterproductive. I know that there is a groundswell of support for self-killing, physician assisted suicide, and euthanasia. Several best-sellers tell stories in which adult children justify their actions in helping their elderly parents commit suicide. These acts are seen as merciful solutions to the problems of suffering and diminishment.

But do we want our doctors and our children ready to kill us? No. I want my doctor to be dedicated to healing me and not opt to finish me off. And the same goes for my children. I don't want them willing to help me commit suicide. In the case of physicians, it is hard enough to establish a trusting relationship, without adding a Dr. Death ingredient to their craft.

I also know that old people can be subtly pressured to give up life by the impatience and inadequacy of their caretakers — or by their own altruistic concerns about the work and expense they are causing their family. When euthanasia is culturally sanctioned, expectations emerge among the elderly that they should not be a burden upon their families and that they should request to die. If families are expected to assist in suicide, impossible conflicts of interest and confusion of roles will ensue. It does not help an adult child to live with the memory of helping to kill his or her old sick parent. As so often happens in our modern societies what starts out as a tragic choice for the rare case can become the routine solution for everyone.

Even if children don't put pressure on the elderly to die, or tactfully suggest this way out, old parents will begin to see currents of public opinion shifting against their taking up of valuable resources. One moves rather quickly from voluntary to involuntary euthanasia. As we have seen in the Netherlands where euthanasia is practiced, abuses creep in once persons start killing others for their own good.

As much I think it wrong to actively prolong dying and to overtreat or engage in futile treatment, it is an overreaction to endorse active killing as a solution. We already have enough killing in this society. Those cultures like ancient Rome and Japan that endorsed suicide were also societies in which there was routine killing of powerless people who got in the way of the more powerful. As Joseph Stalin, a modern exemplar of the total solution, said, "Death solves all problems: no man, no problem." Anyone who may ever be old, weak, and vulnerable, should think twice before giving up our remaining tabus against taking human life. We should try to convince our children and their children that the prohibition against mercy killing protects everyone from the judgments of powerful others who may decide that this one or that one has an unacceptable quality of life. Strong affirmations of the equality of all humans who live lead to affirming the inviolability of each life.

Choosing death ends all choosing. My ability to be a person can be coercively taken from me by death and disease, but how wrong it seems to actively give death a victory on purpose, beforetime. Worse still, giving up in the face of suffering can also become contagious and send a despairing message to one's family.

Parents who commit suicide must know that they are providing models for their grown children. Ernest Hemingway was not alone in killing himself as his father did. One out of four people who attempt suicide has a family member who also tried to commit suicide. I have seen epidemics of suicide among the young— often following another family member's example. When death is seen as the ready and approved way out of suffering, then depressions and defeats will not be struggled against as fiercely. We have always assumed that there is a near invincible biological life force for survival, but this belief may be illusory. The regressive tendency in human beings to give up and die in order to avoid pain may be as strong as the urge to survive. Those who have struggled with a depressed apathetic adult child understands that fatal attractions and deep wells of inertia can pull persons toward nothingness and cessation of consciousness. This pull will become more potent when societies are disrupted and in transition. In America's popular media culture of television and music, death and killing is already omnipresent. When parental authority figures sanction suicide and death by choice, more demoralization will abound.

Another destructive message given by a parent's suicide or request for euthanasia is that we cannot count on others to "see us through." By actively dying through an individual act of will, we are symbolically affirming that no one else can successfully comfort us or accompany us in dying. The interdependence of persons, their mutual care and support is rejected in favor of the ultimate act of technological control. Our survivors will hear the discouraging word; each person is isolated, must die alone and can trust no one for comfort. Surely this will affect the next generation's trust of others. We will be weakening our children's ability to give and receive acts of compassion and comfort.

Better that we ask our children for a steadfast sharing and companionship in our ending. If we are willing to ask for help and receive comfort, we witness to the efficacy of loving bonds between family members. I think in the face of death we should strive for courage and steadfastness, not engage in a rout masquerading as control. Our dying can matter to others who come after us, in more ways than one.

Last Thoughts on the Last Things

Aging well and dying well is my last effort to leave a legacy to my children. I am going before them into this frontier territory. Will I be one of those persons who seems to expand in wisdom and to burn brighter with age? Some older persons do manage to love more, notice more, and enjoy more each day. With little future time left, attention can be focused on the present moment. Mystics and hedonists have learned the art of expansively living in the present moment as in the eternal present. Those old people who reach what has been called "the second naïveté" can be grateful and filled with joy in the world that they must soon leave.

Already I mourn the need to separate from my family and friends. I deeply regret that I must suffer the losses of old age. But an ideal old age and a good death are possible for some. With the help of my children I can still struggle to make my last act a worthy finale.

CHAPTER NINE

Beliefs, Conflicts, and Solidarity

A great and good person can fail as a parent and yet be a success in the larger world. The great Indian leader, Mahatma Gandhi for instance, was not a good father, and other instances of famous people we know come to mind closer to home. A "Mommie Dearest" exposé is a regular feature of our time. In Gandhi's case, his eldest son repudiated his father and all his works, became a Moslem, and lived a dissipated life. Gandhi failed completely in passing on his moral, religious, and political commitments. He knew to the fullest how deeply disappointing it can be when adult children strongly reject their parent's deepest allegiances.

Gandhi sorrowfully recognized that he had "a bad son" prone to moral corruption and ideological rebellion. He explained this outcome as the result of his own blunders, his past evil acts, and his general immaturity when his son was born. His son had been raised poorly, Gandhi explained, because *he* had been away from home so often with his community work. This analysis of parental failure sounds fairly familiar to us, but few American parents would go on to assert as Gandhi did, that Gandhi's evil deeds in an earlier incarnation had also contributed to his son's failures.

But what about individual free will? we protest. Wasn't his son morally responsible for his own choices? I would say yes, but Gandhi took it all upon himself and then concluded, "It is idle to expect one's children and wards necessarily to follow the same course of evolution as oneself."

American parents, however, generally *do* hope that their children will share their moral values as well as their political and religious commitments. It hurts if adult children take a different road in life, while it gladdens the parental heart when they experience solidarity and larger social commitments with their progeny. Almost inevitably a parent's extrafamilial loyalties produce in-family reverberations and expectations. Solidarity of beliefs brings a surge of satisfying unity, and diverging beliefs bring tension and conflict.

Disappointments and Conflicts

An adult child can disappoint and distress a parent in many ways. I have already talked about basic conflicts over work, drug use, sex, money, and reproduction. But these conflicts are not all; it is a further blow when children spurn one's larger moral, political, or religious commitments. This divergence in ideals can happen in two ways.

In its least distressing form, an adult child may take the general tradition he or she was raised in, and push it to a maddening extreme — far, far, beyond the parent's own commitments. The tepid parent may produce an enthusiast, or an enthusiastic parent of either conservative or liberal persuasion may produce a revolutionary fanatic. The moral temperature and the ideological stakes of the family tradition are intensified or turned up to a degree that makes parents uncomfortable and distressed.

In the turbulent sixties we could observe some of these classic family scenarios acted out in politics. Liberal, reforming parents produced revolutionaries and the "Weathermen." Radical children took their parents' democratic commitments to an extreme degree. They were determined not to trust anyone over thirty, and thus could not wait for the establishment to reform the existing system. Children of working class, union members turned to radical red-guard tactics. Sons and daughters of liberal lawyers took up revolutionary violence, building bombs and committing armed robbery for the cause. Two Bryn Mawr graduates, for instance, turned their backs on those ivied halls of reasoned discourse; one ended up in prison, and the other was blown skyhigh in an attempt to build a bomb.

Conservative parents also do not escape the process of their children upping the ante ideologically. They can have children who take the family's conservatism to right-wing extremes. Moderate Republican families can spawn cold warriors who enlist in various wars against liberal corruption. The family tradition of conservative politics takes a qualitative leap when a son or daughter enlists as a follower of Lyndon LaRouche. One set of wealthy parents tried to get their married son judged mentally incompetent so he could be restrained from funneling his inheritance into LaRouche's coffers.

When it comes to religious commitments, parents can be equally ambivalent as their children espouse extreme versions of their own tradition. Assimilated reform Jews with minimal attachment to Judaism have children who, to their surprise, choose to embrace orthodoxy. I know a mother who found her daughter's choice of orthodoxy to be particularly upsetting, because as a lifelong feminist this mother had fought to leave behind what she viewed as the religious constriction of women's lives in that Jewish tradition.

Another reform Jewish mother whose son became an observant orthodox believer experienced regular scoldings from him for her woefully inadequate religious practice. Failures in ritual, dietary observances and worship were deplored. "My son seems to enjoy berating me about my lack of a Kosher kitchen," she said. "That must be one of the joys of his conversion," I replied.

Adult children of Protestant Christian families experience similar discomfort when their children join radical Jesus sects. One mother whose daughter joined a fundamentalist group at college tells a typical tale. These upright parents had taken their children to Sunday school and worshiped regularly at their mainline reformed church. All for nought. In the eyes of their born-again daughter they were deemed remiss in their lukewarm witnessing to Jesus Christ. Their laxness of life and their neglect of daily Bible study and family prayer were patiently pointed out to them. According to their daughter's gospel, only through repentance and stringent witness could they amend their lives.

Anne Tyler, our premier examiner of American family life, spins a similar story in a novel. Ordinary parents from a Protestant tradition are confronted with a son who becomes a superdevout, ardent member of a fundamentalist Christian group. Doug, the father, cannot help feeling distanced from his son: "It was just that Ian seemed — oh, less related to him, somehow. Maybe on account of that born-again business. He belonged to this hole-in-the-wall, born-again church where they called each other Sister and Brother and disapproved of alcohol and sugar and tobacco, disapproved of fun; and Ian at twenty-four seemed more elderly now in some ways than Doug himself."

Prematurely staid, superserious adult children confound their parents. Moderate Catholic parents can also have children who take their Catholicism to an ascetic extreme. Some Catholic parents worry when they see their children espousing evangelical poverty and going to work for the Church in dangerous mission territory. Parents are anxious because idealistic young adults can end up like Jean Donovan, raped and murdered in El Salvador, martyrs to the cause of helping Christ's poor in the Third World. Other young followers of the late radical reformer, Dorothy Day, will give up their careers and take up residence in the urban and rural slums. Like Day, they are often pacifists and peace advocates who may go to jail as a result of illegal protests against military installations.

Strong conservative movements also exist within modern Catholicism that attract young adults to a religious zealotry of the right. A Spanish-founded conservative movement like Opus Dei, for instance, recruits members at elite universities. Parents who are moderate Catholics may have adult children who adopt pre–Vatican II theologies and traditional religious devotions that are different from mainstream American Catholicism. Here again parents can end up being castigated for not being as devout and loyal to their religious commitments as their children think they should be.

True believers are annoying and hard to take whatever their

stripe. But the pain is most acute when an adult child directly repudiates the morality, politics, or religion of his or her parents and embraces an opposing ideology. Politically this happens when offspring of traditional Republicans become radical Democrats or radical liberal parents produce conservative reactionaries. Parents who were dedicated post–World War II Communists rearing their "red diaper babies" can live to see these children vote for Ronald Reagan.

In matters of faith, if I am a devout atheist, I am not overjoyed to see my child become a Catholic, or a Protestant charismatic. An agnostic parent adjusts poorly to his child's proclamations of fundamentalist certitudes. Perhaps a more frequent reversal of direction in secular age is the young adult brought up in a religious family who "loses his faith," and aggressively adopts atheism or agnosticism. Parents who have tried to pass on their religious faith suffer when their adult children renounce their religion. The parents cannot help but mourn the fact that their most cherished beliefs are no longer shared by their children, and in addition they feel that they have failed. Only careless shepherds lose the lambs entrusted to their care.

In an earlier day more children followed their parents in the family faith. In 1955 only 4 percent of the adult population had left the faith of their childhood. By 1985 one-third had. Change and conversion are more the norm in our pluralistic, mobile society.

Some parents are surprised by their child's conversion from the family's Western religion, or from their fervent Western secularism, to a mystical Eastern religion. Since affluent American young people travel far and wide, they find it natural to seek wisdom from other traditions. I know parents whose children went to India and became followers of a Hindu guru. Followers of Middle Eastern Sufi mysticism have outposts in New York City. Ordinary suburban parents can now say, "Meet my daughter the Hare Krishna," or "My son the Buddhist monk." While it is asserted that the practice of Zen Buddhism is compatible with Judeo-Christian religious loyalties, it can seem beyond strange to middle Americans when their child enters a Zen monastery.

Conversions to newer cults are also frequent among adult children who come from nominally religious homes. Many of Sun Moon's followers were raised in assimilated Catholic or Jewish traditions. The definition of a "cult" may be hard to pin down, since admittedly every mainline religion started out as an upstart group. But it is fair to say that a cult is an ultracohesive religious group that is outside the religious mainstream, and includes some unusual practices for ensuring that its members conform to its precepts. Many cults in their efforts to ensure compliance encourage a break with the family of origin, so parents have a special dilemma in dealing with their children who join cults.

I know one set of parents whose daughter had entered a Sun Moon group, and when they sent their son to bring his sister home, he joined as well. This division within the family set in motion decades of struggle; the parents fought to expose what they considered the insidious dangers of the cult, and they struggled to regain the allegiance of their children.

What Should Parents Do about Differences in Belief?

If parents want to remain in close relationships with their adult children, they will keep struggling to maintain communication and to overcome divisive conflicts. Having already invested more than half their life and untold amounts of energy and care, parents don't give up easily. I have already discussed tactics for dealing with parent-child differences over work, money, drugs, sex, reproduction, and life-styles. Political and religious conflicts are somewhat different although the principles of effective communication remain the same in any intergenerational exchange or dialogue. If we assume that parents are fairly good communicators and are going to be respectful, tactful, and collegial as they talk to their adult children, are there different strategies that may serve in different kinds of ideological divisions?

Yes. Surely it makes sense to see that when parent-child differences arise because an adult child has taken the family tradition to an extreme, parents have a ready-made tactic for peacemaking.

They can emphasize the shared heritage and the foundations they and their children still hold in common. The best policy seems to be for parents to affirm everything good that can be observed in the child's extreme position and acknowledge whatever beliefs they can find in common. Emphasizing what one shares in the tradition and avoiding the more divisive issues can reduce tension. It is helpful to look back to the original sources of belief and then trace how, and where, and why, the tradition developed — and where each family member now places himself or herself on the continuum.

Politically parents and children at odds can often stress their patriotic commitment to the country, to the Constitution, to justice and the common good, even if they vociferously disagree over how these commitments should play out in politics. Often it is a particular event that will spark family political fights, and when the specific issue, such as the Gulf War or a Presidential campaign, is over, then a truce can be regained. Even the American Civil War finally ground to a halt for families divided against themselves.

If however, parents and children always find themselves on opposite sides in current political and cultural struggles, then it may become difficult to discuss most political questions. Here we come back to the method of avoidance I recommend in chapter 3. We agree to disagree on certain matters and regularly avoid discussing these contentious issues in the interests of peace. Emphasizing a family consensus on other issues can help. In our contentious family we are all in favor of protecting the environment and working together to save our local woods and waterfront from the developers. As we mutually back off from escalating conflict we can reaffirm our shared convictions.

Passionate family differences over religion can also be managed with an array of strategies. Protestant and Catholic parents subjected to fundamentalist children's crusades may have to work overtime to find the common bonds of their shared heritage. In response to Bible blitzkriegs Christian parents can quote the texts supporting their own interpretations of their faith, or point to the evidence in the gospel that support the claim of an evolutionary development resulting in today's mainline confessions and creeds. Inquiries into how religious authority arises and how it is maintained in a religious group — mine, yours, or theirs — are instructive for every believer. But after defending one's own religious views the best parental strategy, as it so often is, may be to let go, float along, and accept this zealous phase as part of an adult child's spiritual development.

Joining a fundamentalist group often seems to give structure and social support to a young person's life at whatever level of the class structure. In prisons where I have taught, the Moslems are a positive influence bringing a discipline and sense of direction. If a group gives an impetus for a young person to live up to positive ideals in a confusing dissipated culture, then why should parents complain? The great psychoanalyst Anna Freud thought asceticism and intellectualization was the characteristic adolescent defense against internal eruptions of psychic chaos; if true, and if adolescence now lasts until forty, then a young adult is not going to get into too much trouble with his or her fundamentalist asceticism.

If some narrow belief system or dogmatic approach is helping my child to cope or live better, then I am tolerably happy. Besides, youthful periods of dogmatism and ardor often pass or gently subside with more life experience. As someone who in youth harbored my own fanatic tendencies, I can testify that age and hard knocks tend to mellow most true believers. With time, extremists naturally tend to swing back toward the moderate center of their traditions. And if they don't, we may end up admiring their constancy and persistent youthful spirit.

Many good things in people's lives may start off by their going overboard for a while. Political, moral, and religious conversions are a lot like falling in love or suddenly finding inspiration for a life's vocation. Many people who join AA are red-hot converts for a while and bend the ear of everyone on the virtues of the program. After a honeymoon period new loyalties become solidified and people settle down for the long haul. Family and friends who love each other are happy to wait out eruptions of positive enthusiasm.

Paradoxically, some parents like myself often wish that our adult children were more fired up, a little less prudent, balanced, and worldly-wise. After one of my sons launched into an explanation of his sensible, careful plan for preventing stress from overwork, I found myself snapping irritably, " Yes, yes, but whatever happened to giving without counting the cost?" Since aging romantics know themselves to be dangerously slow to reform, I caught myself up quickly. I instantly recanted and allowed as how he was absolutely right to take good care of himself — just as I had always taught him to.

When, however, a child is not just going to extremes, but directly renounces important things in the family tradition, it can be more difficult for parents to keep a positive relationship intact. There will be no common foundation or shared traditional fount to appeal to in discussions. The emotions induced by direct opposition to central parental tenets may be strong and heated. Parents become angry when a child enthusiastically espouses the antithesis of the parent's most cherished beliefs. Ugh! Horrors! How could my child have any truck with this dreadful moral position, political stand, or religious affirmation or denial! Needless to say, canny parents stifle these instinctive reactions of intellectual disgust; they have learned to practice well "the discipline of the tongue," described in chapter 3. Silence and neutral, noncommittal responses are better than howls of disapproval and cascades of criticism and rebuttal.

But even the shrewdest most self-controlled parent can still feel inner arousal — as well as the exhaustion that comes after heroic feats of maintaining their cool under heavy provocation. Perhaps some comfort can be felt by parents who come from rebellious families with a long tradition of intergenerational strife — that fine old American tradition of opposing tradition. In my own family's religious history, my father rebelled against his devout parents, I rebelled against him by returning to the fold, and my children rebelled against me. All I can say is that in such families you belatedly sympathize with what your parents went through, and you look forward to meeting the grandchildren, if there are ever going to be any.

In the meantime parents have to cope with the oppositional dogmas of one's children. It is easier if the ideology adopted is a long-standing worldwide viewpoint, or established religion. However alien it is to me, a worldwide highly developed religion possesses truths and spiritual riches that have nourished its adherents over the centuries. In an established community there will undoubtedly be responsible mentors who can encourage the development of young converts as community members. Every traditional position possesses some truths, and long-standing communities change and develop over time through a succession of creative and corrective internal dialogues. But however ecumenical parents strive to be, it is still the case that an adult child's adoption of some familiar Western belief system will be easier for most American parents to assimilate than, say, a conversion to some foreign superfundamentalism, like becoming a follower of the Ayatollah.

In the end, Gandhi is correct about the individuality and the uniqueness of each person's spiritual and moral evolution. It is clear that no parent can ensure the transference of their own moral affirmations and beliefs to their children. No person can be committed on behalf of another person. Each adult moral and spiritual narrative is self-authored. Once parents accept this fact and really believe it, they can become more tolerant. For one thing they stop blaming themselves for something it is impossible to do — making another person believe and share one's faith. Parents can continue to love and care for their children even if they must disagree with their adherence to what seem egregiously erroneous beliefs.

If I love my adult child and no overt harm is being done, then I can manage to put up with ideas or beliefs that seem wrongheaded and stupid to me. My child is more important to me than the mixed-up ideas that may reside in his or her head at the moment. As I have often remarked about some of my friends and relatives: they are really good people, there is nothing wrong with them but their muddled thinking. Of course they may be saying much the same about me!

It is good for all of us to back off from ideological infallibility.

We can be quite solidly grounded in our own views without being absolutely certain that we are absolutely correct. Haven't we all been wrong before? When we claim only at best a very high probability for the correctness of our views, it is easier to continue a dialogue with those with whom we vigorously disagree. Some absolutist conservative religious groups, and left-wing politically correct movements, practice shunning and repudiation of the dissenter, but it seems a particularly rotten way to run a family.

In the long haul a parent does well to try to be open, to learn all there is to learn and to keep emphasizing the good aspects of a son or daughter's divergent views — without giving up hopes for a change. Engaging occasionally in brief and vigorous critical debates lets us see where we stand. Maybe over time our divergent positions will develop and converge.

But suppose I think that there is nothing that is good and a great deal that is destructive in my child's newfound ideology or group? Certain cults and political movements can seem so authoritarian or so full of brainwashing that its members' moral integrity and/or mental health seem endangered. Think of how the parents felt whose children became followers of James Jones. And there have been other corrupt and charismatic leaders like Bhagwan Shree Rajneeah, "the Rolls Royce Guru" who exploited and gulled his educated followers.

My responsibility to my adult child might induce me to take an actively adversarial position to some cult or organization. This opposition, which I would be open about voicing, could be public and political or privately directed to my adult child. I do not think kidnapping or coerced counterprogramming would ever be morally acceptable; but strenuous countermeasures, short of violence, might be tried in order to effect a rescue, or an exposé.

Could there be any ideological affiliation so morally offensive that parents ought to voluntarily precipitate a break with a child? Maybe. If a mentally competent son or daughter freely joined a racist neo-Nazi party, or adopted Satanism, or took up terrorist violence, could I keep trying to mend our relationship? My son the

Ku Klux Klan member, or my daughter the Libyan assassin, would be repellent. In other conflicts over life-style and morals I have asserted that the parent-child relationship may have to be broken when it is destructive either to the parent or to the child — until, that is, there is some reform of a child's antisocial behavior. Parents now know that they must not be enablers of exploitative behavior when it comes to drugs and crime. If an adult child's ideological affiliation is so destructive of others in society and requires such immoral acts (such as lying, blackmailing, or killing) then a similar break would be in order.

Morality has to be differentiated from religion and politics. Many religious and ideological differences between parents and children do not affect an individual's fundamental commitment to being a morally upright person. Indeed, the sorrow of no longer sharing other larger loyalties can be mitigated when mutual moral respect is maintained. If however, my child were dedicated to and effectively bringing moral evil and violence into the world, I doubt I could manage a civil relationship. I could still love him or her and pray for him or her, but it would be too much of a strain to communicate face to face without trying with every word to counter such destructive work and beliefs.

In less extreme cases where my child or any others are not in danger, or not causing harm to society, but are locked into a narrow ideology, group, church, or cult, then my opposition does not necessitate a break. I recommend treating those family members imprisoned by narrow beliefs as though they were literally imprisoned. In a sense they are in confinement, only in intellectual straitjackets. My job as a parent of such a prisoner is to keep visiting and maintaining family ties and contacts. A family may be the only outsiders a person in a politically correct circle or cult ever meets.

In private family conversations an indoctrinated person hears other points of view aired. Family social events and family bonds can bring diverse individuals together to exchange information and conflicting perspectives. This ability of the family to foster politically incorrect dissent is the reason all totalitarian systems and regimes hate the influence of the family as an institution. The love and affection of one's family group can be a counterforce to larger group pressures and indoctrinations.

Parents and siblings need to try and keep in touch with the family dissenters or true believers using common family bonds to provide links to the mainstream world. Occasionally the wild-eyed eccentrics may be proved right in the future! But even if they aren't, family solidarity is important. We learn to have larger loyalties and commitments through the first bonds and moral obligations we accept for immediate kin and clan. We learn to love and care for humanity at large by caring for those persons we know in particular. With some few exceptions, I think parents ought to strive to remain in communication and stay attentive and involved with their adult children, no matter how saddened the parents are over the child's rejection of parental beliefs.

Parental Compensation

If a parent has suffered family opposition and the defection of adult children from one's cherished beliefs there are some compensatory strategies to be undertaken. Whatever ongoing community a parent belongs to, there will be young people in it who need mentors. Many a parent has been forced to conclude, "If my own children won't listen, I can still help other young people who believe as I do." Parental beliefs and commitments will be stronger for having been winnowed and tested by intra-family struggle. A middle-aged parent's commitments to a larger community or to a cause can give him or her sustenance in life, whether his or her children come along or not.

While Gandhi's failures with his sons were grievous to him, he also had many, many spiritual sons and daughters and a multitude of disciples and coworkers. As he saw it, his pain and disappointment over his private family failures should not deter him from his call to work for truth and the liberation of his country. It is also true that ordinary parents may have young friends and protégés outside the family who can benefit from the wisdom the parent has to offer. This can give a parent a sense of generativity and the satisfaction of passing on his or her deepest beliefs, even if one's adult children are not interested.

Only one caution is in order in the matter of young protégés outside the family. A delicate situation may arise when like-minded young adults the age of one's adult children share a parents ideals, values, and particular causes. A mentoring relationship is well and good, but I have seen parents who made it fairly clear to all and sundry that they valued their young colleagues and protégés more than their own children who were disappointing to them. In the young favorites the parents claimed the ideal son or daughter they wished they had produced, a spiritual child, more of an equal, who could admire and be more receptive to the parent's accomplishments. A fictive sibling rivalry can be developed between child and protégé.

For a parent either to encourage or indulge in such symbolic sibling rivalry seems wrong. A good parent should strive to put his or her child first, and emphasize that there is always a special place for one's son or daughter that is not dependent on competitive achievements or perfect ideological compatibility. One's child does not have to be one's disciple. A parent can have many young friends and colleagues, but only one relationship with a child. It is difficult enough to manage actual sibling rivalries in a family without introducing competition from others. In the end, commitments to loving partiality and immutable lifetime preference should be an essential part of the good parent's role.

The Joys of Parent-Child Solidarity

When parents look at their newborns and toddlers they do not think about the fact that for decades they and their children will be fellow citizens. When there is family solidarity and shared convictions parents and children can find themselves working together in political campaigns and causes. The idea of producing like-minded fellow voters is far from the new parent's mind. Yet parents who produce children on the same wavelength ideologically can look forward to decades of cooperation in civic and religious life. Parents and adult children may work together in the environmental movement, in political parties, and in many other volunteer endeavors. Parents and adult children can teach Sunday school together and worship in the same church.

Happy the parents whose grown children share their moral, political, and religious allegiances! Parents want their children to be like them, only slightly better, or even slightly different — within an acceptable range, or close enough for comfort. Kinship, friendship, ideals, and commitments can merge in a family and when it happens it produces a particular and intense form of parental satisfaction. Good God, these admirable young persons are the fruit of my womb, or my loins, and partially the result of my nurturance. With sons and daughters who are soul mates a parent can have a deep, rich sense of unity. Conversation can be free and unbridled, ranging over a panoply of shared interests. To me the most valid measure of the quality of life can be found in the level of the conversations you have; when your children provide wonderful talk, then family life is a joy.

In conversational give-and-take, parents have the instructive experience of learning from their adult children. Mothers apparently are more influenced by their adult children than fathers, but this must be a function of who talks most frequently with whom in a family. Both fathers and mothers have found out innumerable new things through sharing their children's interests and concerns. In my own case the children educated me to the energy crisis and the need for ecological awareness and conservation. Somehow my optimistic generation of Americans had received the message that all resources were endlessly available. Never having heard the word "ecology," or "feedback," we had no sense that elements in the environment were interrelated. Systems thinking and concepts of side effects and recursive feedback loops had not yet been invented. In my youth when I looked at smokestacks billowing black soot into the air, I would admire the beautiful patterns traced against the sky. Our children's green generation has attuned us to the need for clean air, clean water, and open space.

Parents and adult children can enlarge each others vision of the world. Happily, families talk, argue, and educate each other in the process.

EPILOGUE

Parents Forever

Parents of adults find themselves engaged in an ongoing journey within a collective family network. Today parents and children have longer to live together than ever before, in some cases over sixty years. But the technological advances that give parents their longer life expectancy also make the parental task more difficult and prolonged. Much more education of offspring is necessary for a child to become a self-sufficient adult. Our society also contains more pluralistic beliefs and more cultural turbulence that make it difficult to pass on parental values to the next generation.

In bad economic times parental help becomes more necessary and more prolonged as young adults struggle to make it. One result of this can be positive: Adult children who hang around home longer and get more help will be more grateful and more involved with their parents. Parent-child friendships have more chance of flourishing than in the preceding postwar generations. Family ties between parents and late maturing children can be closer. In any event, intimacy and family bonds between parents and adult children generally increase over the life span as children mature.

In a time of seismic cultural shifts there may, however, be new arenas of conflict undreamed of in an earlier time. I have talked of many of the ways that parents were not prepared, and could not have been prepared, for the surprising differences between an America of the fifties and the America of the nineties. In different chapters I have detailed the new questions and conflicts that can come up in regard to work, sex, reproduction, morality, religion, and so on. While there is greater potential for positive satisfactions in today's parenting, there is also more chance for crises and tragedies. Family life can be a high-risk, high-gain enterprise with devastating losses to drugs, mental illness, and suicide.

By the time one's children are nearing forty they are poised on the brink of middle age and their parents are facing old age. They are both in middle adulthood enjoying the precious equilibrium of power that characterizes the extended time in the middle of the lengthened life cycle. But family life isn't over yet. There is no discernible finishing line or final goal for parental investment of emotions and commitment to their children. When the family drama plays well, its run is an extended one. Giving and receiving, parents and their adult children can continue to care for each other as long as they live. Reciprocity between the generations has always been the law of culture and family life, and it still is, although taking new forms.

The increased understanding of psychological processes makes living in a family today a more self-conscious enterprise. We know more about the tendency of maladaptive family patterns to perpetuate themselves and this gives us a new ability to intervene and change ourselves for the better. A child who was abused does not *have* to grow up to be an abuser. The much discussed "dysfunctional family" of "codependents" does not have to remain so. While there is a lot of psychological jargon abroad in the land, and concepts like "enabling" and "toughlove" can always be abused, I think American families are better off for being more sophisticated and self-conscious. Perhaps in simpler times a completely intuitive form of parental behavior would serve, but today we have to meet complex new problems and be more reflective and prudent about our actions and reactions. What is a family and what is its purpose? Thinking about these things can make us more appreciative of the opportunity to love and to serve our kin and to be loved and helped in turn.

Together throughout the life cycle parents and children fulfill the traditional role of all families as a shield against misfortune and a buffer against the blows of fate. At all times good or bad, families matter to each other and give meaning to life by their partiality and preference for the faces, the familiar persons who are more important to me, and I to them, than all the swirling mass of strangers. In hard times, like wars and depressions, actual survival may depend on family bonds and cooperation. Family networks can be latent and then in emergencies emerge to offer support.

But affluent families in good time can also have their own crises. When the larger culture challenges and rejects the moral assumptions upon which families are founded, each family has to fight to maintain moral standards and meet its moral obligations. Yet at the same time certain constancies exist for all parents of adults. Young adult children are going to succeed them, and since there is diversity in adult families there may also be conflict, incompatibility, and sibling rivalry to surmount. Individuals in a family choose their own moral path despite pressures from the environment predisposing them to be either good or ill.

Over and over I have made the point that a mentally competent adult child is a free moral agent and is in charge of who he or she becomes. Parents are not omnipotent and cannot control what happens to their children. Parents can, however, control their own actions in how they live, and how they give or withhold whatever resources they have. The delicate parental challenge with adult children that is touched on in many different chapters is how to give help in the best possible way, or how to avoid encouraging immaturity and dependence. Different ways to run an adult family and household(s) have been described, each with advantages and disadvantages. Clearly my own preference is for separate private households living near one another in a cooperative family network engaging in a great deal of close communication. I also recognize that this ideal will take longer to achieve today and that there is more variety in adult life-styles than ever before. Fortunately, some institutions help the family manage today, such as retirement communities and half-way houses for those who are mentally impaired. A family can make use of an institution without abandoning family care, emotional commitment, contact, and communication.

Conversing is the main way of relating in a family of adults who are independent. Learning the art of being friends, and friendly talk, takes some readjustment for many parents. I have offered my good friend test, and given ways to handle inevitable family conflicts. I believe in the discipline of the tongue, tact, and avoidance for the sake of peacekeeping, enlivened by a quick clean skirmish from time to time.

In my discussions of work, sex, reproduction, tragedies, and preparing for old age I take opinionated positions on particular conflicts that parents face. I am dubious about sexual permissiveness, but in favor of gender equality and acceptance of homosexuality. I'm in favor of grandchildren, against third-party reproduction, in favor of adoption, and sympathetic with the new complexities of reproduction facing this generation. I hate the thought of old age and dying but think we must prepare ourselves and our children, without euthanasia. I hope readers who disagree with my opinions will have at least been stimulated to further develop their own convictions.

Obviously, I could never get around to covering each parent's particular, thorny problem. There is more material left out than included. My main purpose in this book has been to offer a reflective critique, a framework, and to try and reassure parents of adults that they are not alone in their struggles — or in their satisfactions. Young adulthood is now being defined as a new and different stage in the life cycle that needs more attention. Families have been sent reeling as they have tried to cope with their young adults and the society's constricted economic expectations. Downward mobility is as much a fact of American life as the ideological assaults upon family commitments. Yet those observers who from time to time predict the demise of family ties will always be confounded by the strength and staying power of the psychological bonds between parents and their children.

While I have given full weight and a lot of words to discussions of crises and conflicts, I am basically an optimist about family life. Adult children mature and stop blaming their parents for earlier mistakes that their parents may have made. A grown-up person begins to see that there is something absurd about avoiding responsibility for one's own future by complaining about what others did in the past. Parents for their part can learn gracefully to give up critical nagging, exaggerated expectations, and entrenched habits of directing family traffic. Parents and children can together retire illusions of perfection, and simply be grateful that they still have each other. After being together for decades on the family voyage, each one can realize that "through many dangers, toils and snares we have already come." Many families have been through misfortunes, tragedies, and dreadful sieges of pain as well as happy times. After being knocked about in various storms, each calm day is appreciated.

I am convinced that perseverance and patience are as important to cultivate as the traditional virtues of justice, prudence, courage, and moderation. Perhaps only recurring infusions of the gifts of hope and love can provide the parental energy to keep traveling on the common journey. Stubbornness also helps. We set out to form a family and a family we shall be, despite all odds and obstacles. Perfect success is not possible or necessary, but parents are morally required to pay attention and stay the course. This commitment to parenthood is, for the most part, faithfully carried out, year after year — indeed it continues forever.

Selected Bibliography

For readers who want to know more here is a brief, selected list of books that will lead you further into the issues raised in this book:

Anderson, Patricia. *Affairs in Order: A Complete Resource Guide to Death and Dying*. New York: Macmillan, 1991.

Bellah, Robert N., Richard Madsen, William M. Sullivan, Ann Swidler, and Steven M. Tipton. *Habits of the Heart: Individualism and Commitment in American Life*. Berkeley: University of California Press, 1981.

Bernheim, Kayla F., Richard R. J. Lewine, and Caroline T. Beale. *The Caring Family: Living with Chronic Mental Illness*. New York: Random House, 1982.

Blankenhorn, David, Steven Bayme, and Jean Bethke Elshtain, eds. *Rebuilding the Nest: A New Commitment to the American Family*. Milwaukee: Family Service America, 1990.

Blustein, Jeffrey. *Parents & Children: The Ethics of the Family*. New York: Oxford University Press, 1982.

Callahan, Sidney. *In Good Conscience: Reason and Emotion in Moral Decision Making*. San Francisco: HarperSanFrancisco, 1991.

D'Emilio, John, and Estelle B. Freedman. *Intimate Matters: A History of Sexuality in America*. New York: Harper & Row, 1988.

Francoeur, Robert T., ed. *Taking Sides: Clashing Views on Controversial Issues in Human Sexuality*. Guilford, Conn.: Dushkin Publishing Group, 1991.

Gross, Zenith Henkin. *And You Thought It Was All Over!: Mothers and Their Adult Children*. New York: St. Martin's Press, 1985.

Gutmann, David. *Reclaimed Powers: Toward a New Psychology of Men and Women in Later Life*. New York: Basic Books, 1987.

Hetherington, E. Mavis, and Josephine D. Arasteh, eds. *Impact of Divorce, Single Parenting, and Stepparenting on Children*. Hillsdale, N.J.: Lawrence Erlbaum Associates, 1988.

Hochschild, Arlie. *Second Shift: Working Parents and the Revolution at Home*. New York: Viking, 1989.

Lancaster, Jane B., Jeanne Altmann, Alice S. Rossi, and Lonnie R. Sherrod, eds. *Parenting across the Life Span: Biosocial Dimensions*. New York: Aldine De Gruyter, 1987.

LeMasters, E. E., and John DeFrain. *Parents in Contemporary America: A Sympathetic View*. 5th ed. Belmont, Calif.: Wadsworth, 1989.

Longman, Phillip. *Born to Pay: The New Politics of Aging in America*. Boston: Houghton Mifflin, 1987.

O'Neill, Onora, and William Ruddick, eds. *Having Children: Philosophical and Legal Reflections on Parenthood*. New York: Oxford University Press, 1979.

Pifer, Alan, and Lydia Bronte, eds. *Our Aging Society: Paradox and Promise*. New York: W. W. Norton, 1986.

Popenoe, David. *Disturbing the Nest: Family Change and Decline in Modern Societies*. New York: Aldine de Gruyter, 1988.

Rossi, Alice S., and Peter H. Rossi. *Of Human Bonding: Parent-Child Relations across the Life Course*. New York: Aldine De Gruyter, 1990.

Skolnick, Arlene. *Embattled Paradise: The American Family in an Age of Uncertainty*. New York: Basic Books, 1991.

Tannen, Deborah, Ph.D. *You Just Don't Understand: Women and Men in Conversation*. New York: Ballantine Books, 1990.

Weitzman, Lenore J. *The Divorce Revolution*. New York: Free Press, 1985.

Yankelovich, Daniel. *New Rules: Searching for Self-Fulfillment in a World Turned Upside Down*. New York: Random House, 1981.

Zuckerman, Connie, J.D., Nancy Neveloff Dubler, Ll.B., and Bart Collopy, Ph.D., eds. *Home Health Care Options: A Guide for Older Persons and Concerned Families*. New York: Plenum Press, 1990.